Introduct

Hay-on-Wye, or **Y Gelli**, is an unus of the spectacular Brecon Beacons N bookshops its primary function was came in from surrounding areas to buy and sell stock. ponies from the hills through the narrow streets of the town. Now it clearly deserves its title of Book Town, as there are numerous bookshops – and also an increasing number of artisans trading in the town. Furthermore, Hay is a *Walkers are Welcome* town and has an annual Walking Festival, as well as the world famous Literary Festival and a Bike Festival, so tourism is now embedded in the town's make up; thousands come to enjoy these events.

Hay was at one time a major crossing point of the River Wye and has had a turbulent history: Hay castles (there were two) are reminders of this period of repression and conflict during the early Norman period. In the 19thC the town settled to an agrarian existence. The arrival of the railway from Hereford in 1864 provided the wherewithal to transport local produce east; it was known as the Egg and Bacon line!

What makes Hay-on-Wye so appealing is the exceptional diversity of landscapes, from the serenity of the Wye to the etched outlines of the Black Mountains and the Brecon Beacons. There's also a rich rural culture; take for example the writings of the Reverend Francis Kilvert, or the photography of Alfred Watkins about the area. In this book, several walks feature Hay itself, but there are as many in the Golden Valley, a few miles to the east. It is one of the quietest corners of Herefordshire and the foothills leading to the Black Mountains are magical. Almost each and every settlement has a castle mound and Norman church situated nearby, a reflection of harsher medieval times. Now these places are sleepy enclaves, many of which have good footpath networks that are walked, but not by many.

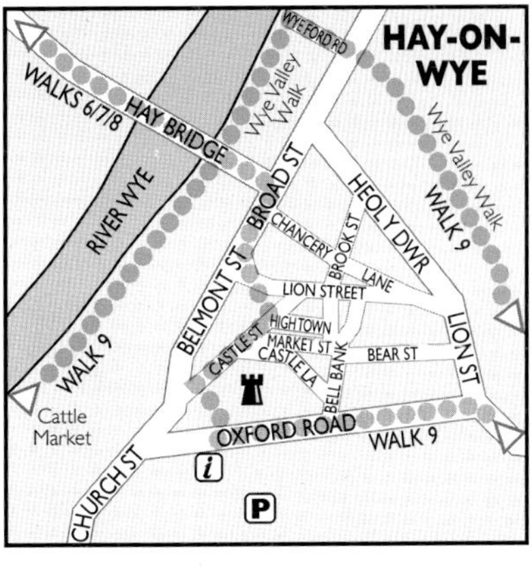

Hay-on-Wye is served by a bus (39/39A/39B) from Hereford Railway Station and Brecon. If you are unsure about a bus or train time it is best to contact 'traveline' or 'traveline cymru' in Wales – 0171 200 2233 – for buses and 'National Rail Enquiries' – 08457 484950 – for train times.

Enjoy your walks!

TWO WALKS FROM TALGARTH

DESCRIPTION Talgarth is a pleasant little market town about halfway between Hay and Brecon. It's worth visiting for its own sake, not least because of the restored Talgarth Mill, with its working water-powered mill, bakery, café and craft shop (all currently shut on Mondays). These two walks give an introduction to the surrounding countryside. **Walk 1** (3 miles) allows a gentle exploration of the Llynfi Valley to the west of Talgarth, with superb views across to the Black Mountains, and a visit to Bronllys Castle. The path between Tregunter and Bronllys can get flooded in very wet weather. **Walk 2** (5 miles) takes you east of the town closer to the mountains and through Park Wood, an attractive hillside wood, formerly managed by the Forestry Commission but now owned by the Woodland Trust; it is gradually being de-coniferised so that its ancient woodland features can be protected and restored. There's a short steep climb up through the wood, but the rest of the walk isn't strenuous. Talgarth is now a 'Walkers are Welcome' town and has a popular walking festival each year in May. A good selection of longer walks from Talgarth is available from the Tourist Information and Resource Centre in the Square. **START** Talgarth Mill, The Square, Talgarth SO 155338

DIRECTIONS There's a direct bus service (39/39B) from Hereford, Hay-on-Wye or Brecon to Talgarth about once every two hours on Mondays-Saturdays, with two buses per day (39A) on Sundays. The bus stops in the Square. There is parking available at the old station car park in Talgarth, situated off the High Street.

WALK 1 – BRONLLYS CASTLE & THE RIVER LLYNFI

1 From the entrance to Talgarth Mill go LEFT along High Street ahead to reach a roundabout. Keep on the RIGHT hand side to cross the road to the entrance of Gwernyfed RFC. Go through a kissing gate, along a lane through a bridle gate by a barn. Head diago-

nally across the field, cross a stile and continue over a bridge and stile. Keep ahead through a gateway to go left at a junction. Cross a stile by a gate onto a road.

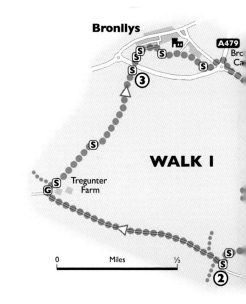

2 Turn RIGHT, cross a bridge, and rise on the road to Tregunter farm. Just after the farmhouse go RIGHT through a gate, ahead by the barns to cross a stile. Continue ahead and the path dips to cross the stream across a footbridge. Cut RIGHT through wet ground to cross a stile to a hedge. Follow this as it bends left continuing along it but as you approach another hedge aim slightly LEFT through a gap and continue in a similar direction in the next field then down to a footbridge. Go over it to cross a stile. The path cuts RIGHT and up to the road. Cross with care.

3 The path bends LEFT to cross a stile into a field. Head slightly LEFT to cross a stile into a school field. Walk ahead through a gate onto a road. Go RIGHT on a path which bends LEFT by bungalows and by the site of a moat. At the end go RIGHT over a stile and curve to the LEFT. Go through a gap in a hedge and continue to the bottom left corner. Cross a stile and aim slightly RIGHT to cross another onto a road verge. Cross over and turn RIGHT to cross the bypass. Continue ahead towards Talgarth whereupon you come across the castle keep at Bronllys.

4 Continue ahead to a group of houses on the opposite side at Castle Green. Go RIGHT across the road (at signpost); walk down a track through two bridle gates, go RIGHT and then LEFT to cross a stile into a field. Keep ahead to go over a tractor track and then

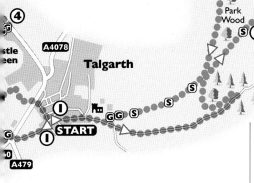

LEFT through a bridle gate. Follow the riverside path through another gate; in the next field look for a footbridge on the LEFT. Cross this and walk slightly RIGHT, through a barred gate then ahead in the next field. Go through a kissing gate into the grounds then ahead to a road by housing. Turn RIGHT, passing the pavilion and then follow the lane to the LEFT. As it bends left go ahead across the road and walk alongside the River Ennig; cut LEFT across the footbridge and RIGHT back to the Square.

WALK 2 – PARK WOOD

I From the entrance to Talgarth Mill, turn RIGHT and RIGHT again up The Bank. Bear RIGHT into Church Street to pass the church. Take the second LEFT fork, signed to Park Wood. After passing Park Cottage, the road enters the wood. Take the first turning on the LEFT by a sign for Park Wood. Walk past a gate and follow the path. Ignore two right turns and when a waymarked path crosses the track turn RIGHT quite steeply uphill. At the top cross a larger track and very soon leave the wood over a stile.

2 Turn LEFT along the field edge and soon bear slightly RIGHT next to bracken. At the end of the field, keep ahead on the path close to the fence on the left, crossing one stile, then another. Turn RIGHT in front of an old broken fence (in 2014), and follow the fence to cross a stile ahead and then another into a small patch of bracken. The path then re-enters woodland over a stile. Bear RIGHT to follow the track, and leave the woodland over a stile. Go straight ahead over pasture and bear RIGHT to pick up a track going into a farmyard through a gate. Keep ahead through farm buildings and follow the tarmac road as it bends to LEFT and RIGHT out of the farm.

3 At a T junction, turn LEFT and at once leave the road to walk ahead along a track. Follow this, passing a house over to the right, until the track turns right. Here turn LEFT through a gate. Keep next to the fence on the right at first, then, when the fence turns right, leave it by continuing ahead, towards trees in front of you. At a telegraph pole, bear LEFT towards a stile. Cross this into Bradwys Wood. Ignore paths to right and left until you reach the cross paths where you turned up through the wood earlier. Here turn RIGHT, soon going down steps. Leave the wood over a stile and walk down fields towards Talgarth in front of you, crossing two more stiles and leaving the last field through a gate. Turn RIGHT through another and walk down to re-join the road back past the church.

WALK 3

THE TWMPA

DESCRIPTION The Twmpa (also known as Lord Hereford's Knob) is one of the well-known peaks of the Black Mountains. It's by no means the highest at 689 metres, but as this walk starts from river level you'll be climbing about 600 metres, and it's quite a strenuous climb. Most people ascend the Twmpa from a car park fairly near the top on the other side, but the route from Glasbury is much quieter and will give you a real sense of achievement as you see the top getting closer and closer. The total distance of this walk is 9½ miles. Before or after the walk you may like to visit the River Café, currently shut on Mondays and Tuesdays but otherwise open all day; to get there follow the road round to the left towards Hereford from the bus stop; the café is on the right before the river.

START Glasbury Bridge bus stop SO 181391.

DIRECTIONS There's a direct bus service (39/39B) from Hereford, Hay-on-Wye or Brecon to Glasbury about once every two hours on Mondays-Saturdays, with two buses per day (39A) on Sundays. There is a very small car park on the west side of Glasbury Bridge.

1 Walk away from the river up a minor road (signed towards Tregoed and Felindre) next to the bus shelter. Walk under an old bridge, then almost at once turn LEFT over a stile down into a field next to a house. Turn half RIGHT across the field, passing a large oak tree on your left, to a gate leading onto a road. Turn LEFT and walk up the road. In a few minutes, after passing the last building on the left, turn RIGHT through a gate into a meadow. Keep RIGHT along the hedge to enter a wood through a gate. Ignore left turns and leave the wood through another gate and a little later a third one onto a road. Turn LEFT.

2 Immediately turn RIGHT through a gate. Turn half LEFT across the field to a gate, go through it, cross the road and go through another gate to walk just to the left of a house. By now the Twmpa is clearly in view straight ahead of you. Keep to the right

of a line of telegraph poles to leave the field over a stile in the corner. Turn RIGHT over the stream and at once LEFT next to the stream. Soon turn RIGHT through a gate into a garden. Follow the path round to the LEFT close to the stream and leave the garden through a gate. Another gate takes you into the next field. Here you head slightly RIGHT away from the stream to a stile into the next field. Keep ahead here and slightly LEFT to a small gate (with a large one each side of it) leading onto a road.

3 Cross the road to enter the next field over a stile. Walk straight ahead, climb another stile by a gate and keep to the left side of the field until you get to a stile on the left. Don't cross it, but turn RIGHT here and then half RIGHT again to walk across the field towards an old barn. To the left of the barn is a stile; cross this onto a road and turn LEFT. The route climbs (with a few little dips) for about a mile, then crosses a cattle grid onto open land.

4 Continue on the road until it turns right. Leave it by bearing LEFT here at a post along a rough track, soon approaching a fence on your left. When the fence turns sharp left, keep ahead on the track, soon following it round to the LEFT across a stream. About 15 yards after the stream fork RIGHT up a smaller track. This gradually bends round to the left and joins another coming in from the right. A little later it curls round to the RIGHT in a large U turn and goes on up the hillside, now going away from the summit. It joins another path coming in from the left and eventually reaches the ridge.

5 Here turn sharply LEFT along the ridge, soon bearing RIGHT up the final ascent to the cairn on top. When you've had a good rest and admired the view, retrace your steps to the rocky outcrop where you joined the ridge and turn sharp RIGHT downhill. When the path forks take the LEFT hand one. Just after the U-turn round to the LEFT, turn RIGHT down a grassy track. At the bottom you will see, going from left to right, a fence line dotted with trees. Aim for the right hand corner, where the fence turns left to go away from you. When you get there, follow the fence on your left down and through a gate. The route continues in the same direction through a gate and then, by a farm, two more. Just after the farm there is a stile/gate on the left and just beyond this on the left is the little 18thC Penyrheol Baptist Chapel, in a beautifully peaceful setting.

6 The road down continues in the same direction, eventually going along the edge of Tregoyd Common. It bends sharply to the right to a cattle grid. Immediately in front of the cattle grid, turn LEFT over a stile and walk straight down the field to another stile leading to a road. Cross the road and the stile the other side of it and bear LEFT, heading for trees down to the RIGHT. Near the bottom of the field, go RIGHT over a footbridge with a stile at each end, then cross another stile onto a stony track. Turn LEFT. Pass through a gate and follow the track through buildings; then bear RIGHT to a road. Go straight across and ahead along the road opposite. At the next junction again go straight ahead, this time through a gate onto a lane. Follow this through another gate and enter a wood. At a cross tracks ignore turnings to right and left and continue to descend and leave the wood through a gate into a meadow. Bear left to pass a mound of trees and rejoin the track you came along earlier. Return to the gate onto a road and then proceed back into Glasbury.

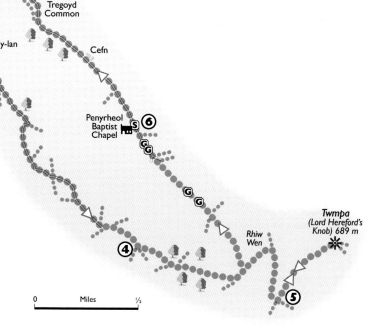

WALK 4

LLOWES

DESCRIPTION A moderate 4½ mile walk to the village of Llowes passing a fine Welsh chapel at Maesyronnen. The route climbs into the foothills above the Wye floodplain to cross Cilcenni Dingle, managed by the Woodland Trust and home to diverse flora and fauna. Your target is the small village of Llowes which has two landmarks, the church of St Meilig, dating from medieval times, but essentially Victorian, and the Radnor Arms, a roadside inn of old.

START & FINISH River Café, Glasbury SO 181392.

DIRECTIONS There's a direct bus service (39/39B) from Hereford, Hay-on-Wye or Brecon to Glasbury about once every two hours on Mondays-Saturdays, with two buses per day (39A) on Sundays. From the bus stop follow the road round to the left towards Hereford; the café, currently shut on Mondays and Tuesdays but otherwise open all day, is on the right before the river. There is a very small car park on the west side of Glasbury Bridge.

1 From the entrance to the River Café turn RIGHT across the bridge over the River Wye to join the Wye Valley Walk. The bridge looks pretty solid now but many earlier structures failed to survive floods and an old ferry was re-instated on more than one occasion. Go RIGHT down steps and through a gate into a field and proceed ahead by a sewage works (no need to hold your noses here however!). Pass beneath the poplar trees to slip through a kissing gate into the next pasture and then through another gate soon after. *To the left you'll see Maesllwch Castle (not open to the public), a house re-built in the mid 19thC and exhibiting a curious mix of architectural styles, amid extensive parkland. This is on the site of an earlier ancient manor.* Mid-way along the field head slightly LEFT across it to pass through two gates in succession to the main road.

2 Turn RIGHT to walk along the wide verge but in just over 100 yards cross over (with care) to walk up a lane signposted to Capel Maesyronnen. Pass by the lodge and climb steeply up to the turn for Maesyronnen farm on the left. Turn next RIGHT at the junction for Maesyronnen Chapel. *This is said to be the oldest unaltered nonconformist chapel in Wales dating from 1697. It was built using the framework of an earlier building, a barn, and some argue that it had been used as a meeting place for dissenters in earlier times. The chapel is still used as a place of worship and next door is a cottage owned by the Landmark Trust – a beautiful place to stay.* By the chapel and cottage, go LEFT through a barred gate, up the field to exit by way of a stile at the top. *There are great views back over to the Black Mountains so it might be an idea to pause awhile to savour them.* Turn RIGHT on the road and as this bends left, go RIGHT over a stile on the right by a barred gate.

3 Proceed down the field to cross another stile into Cilcenni Dingle. The well worn path winds down, through wet patches and tumbling over tree roots, to a footbridge across a stream. It then climbs up steps, across a path and ahead to a stile. Cross it and walk slightly RIGHT up the field towards Gaer farm. Cross a stile in the next boundary and head slightly RIGHT towards the farm.

4 Climb a stile onto the lane and go LEFT for a few yards and then RIGHT on the track and RIGHT again through a gate into a small enclosure by the buildings and then onward through another gate. Head slightly LEFT across a field to a barred gate about 20 yards to the left of a corner. Once through continue ahead with a hedge to your right, but then ease LEFT towards a stream and proceed through a barred gate where the ground can be wet in winter. Continue ahead near to the stream to cross a stile by a gate and ahead once again in the next pasture. Before reaching the far bottom corner gate look for a stile on the LEFT. Cross this and a plank bridge across the stream to the highway.

5 Go RIGHT to pass by the old Zion Chapel and soon after pass Moity Farm. Stay on this road for a little over half a mile; just after

6

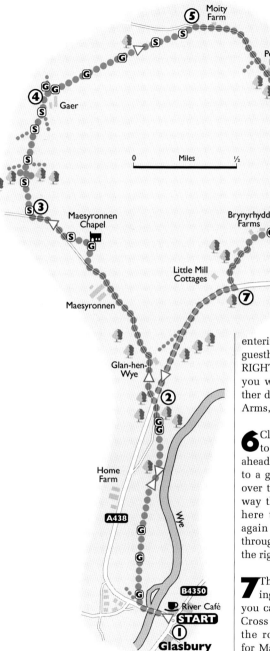

entering the village of Llowes pass Westview guesthouse on the left. In 30 yards or so, turn RIGHT to join the Wye Valley Walk, unless you want to visit the church, which is further down the road on the left, or the Radnor Arms, which is at the bottom of the road.

6 Climb over a stile and pass through a gate to walk through two enclosures and then ahead in a field. The path rises up the bank to a gate and into woodland, but look back over the village first. A clear path winds its way through the wood to a track. Go LEFT here to pass Brynyrhydd farm and LEFT again by barns to drop down the hillside, through a gate and with an old millhouse to the right in Cilcenni Dingle.

7 The bad news is there's a section of walking along the road verge, but it is wide so you can avoid the worst of the traffic noise. Cross over and turn RIGHT to walk along the roadside border back to the junction for Maesyronnen and to the kissing gate by a signpost which you passed on the outbound section. Retrace your steps back into Glasbury in time for tea.

GLASBURY TO HAY-ON-WYE

DESCRIPTION This is a varied 5 mile linear walk. It starts by going across country from the river Wye at Glasbury to the attractive village of Llanigon, and then ascends through woodland, with good views at the top over to Hay and the western side of the Wye Valley. Finally it descends to Hay through an unspoilt area of common land. There is one steep climb; the rest of the walk is undemanding.

START Glasbury Bridge bus stop SO 181391.

FINISH Hay Castle bus stop and car park, Oxford Road, Hay-on-Wye SO 230422..

DIRECTIONS There's a direct bus service (39/39B) from Hereford, Hay-on-Wye or Brecon to Glasbury about once every two hours on Mondays-Saturdays, with two buses per day (39A) on Sundays

▌ After getting off the bus, you may wish to look at the river before starting the walk. Follow the path next to the main road towards Hereford round to the left and you will soon be on the bridge. You will also pass the popular River Café, currently open all day except on Mondays and Tuesdays. Then return to the bus stops. Walk away from the river up a minor road (signed to Tregoed and Felindre) next to the bus shelter. Walk under an old bridge, then almost at once turn LEFT over a stile down into a field next to a house.

Turn half RIGHT across the field, passing a large oak tree on your left, to a gate leading onto a road. Turn LEFT, and walk along the road for 10 – 15 minutes.

2 When the road divides into two, bear LEFT, then after a few steps turn RIGHT onto a track. Soon cross a footbridge and go through a gate. Follow the track into the trees, soon entering a field where you bear LEFT to walk along the left hand edge of the field. Keep ahead through a gate and, later, another. Pass a gate on the left and turn LEFT almost at once through a second gate. Keep next to the hedge on the right through two fields to a gate. Once through this, carry on close to the fence on the right above the wood. Eventually the path leaves the fence, passing a large flat stone, to descend ahead slightly to the left. (Ignore the smaller track forking right up to the fence.) When the path ends at a lane, turn LEFT.

3 The lane makes a U-turn to the RIGHT to take you next to the stream for a while, then emerges from the wood and winds down through a gate towards the main road.

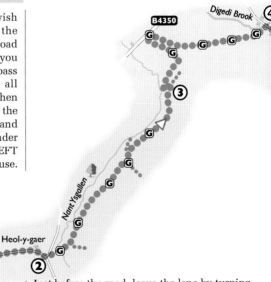

Just before the road, leave the lane by turning RIGHT through a gate. Walk diagonally LEFT across the field to a gate just to the left of the far corner. Go through this, then ahead and slightly RIGHT across a little ditch to another gate. Once through this, keep ahead in the same direction to, and through, a gate just to the left of the garden next to a large bunga-low. Cross a footbridge and follow the path through trees and past a house on your left to reach a road. Turn RIGHT to walk into the pretty village of Llanigon.

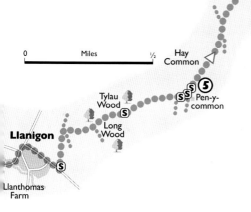

Cross a stile, then very soon turn LEFT over another and then a third, which takes you onto Hay Common, an area of common land which feels quite remote but is actually less than a mile from Hay-on-Wye.

5 You can wander at will over the Common, but for the most direct route keep near the left hand edge downhill, through alternating patches of woodland and pasture. After several of these you find your-self walking with a fence not just on your left but also on your right. You then emerge into a flatter area of grassland with a gate over to the left. Now stay close to the fence/hedge on your RIGHT and you're eventually funnelled down to the bottom end of the common, with two gates in front of you.

6 Go through the right hand one and walk straight ahead across a field to pass through an old gateway, then ahead and slightly RIGHT to approach a fence on your left. Keep near the LEFT side of this field, through another gateway ahead and on towards the right of a grey barn. Go through a gate and bear LEFT down a short track to a road. Turn LEFT and at once leave the road to the RIGHT of railings along a path. Follow this through a gate, walk past a gate on your left and continue past a small indus-trial estate. Another gate ahead and a foot-bridge take you into a field. Bear LEFT close to the left hand hedge and finally another gate takes you into the car park, at the top of which are the bus stops.

4 The road crosses the Digedi Brook. Shortly after this, at a junction, continue straight ahead, signed towards Hay-on-Wye, but very soon turn RIGHT by The Old Forge garage. About 30 metres after the speed limit sign, opposite a gateway, turn LEFT up steps and over a stile. Stay next to the fence/hedge on your left until you reach a stile ahead. Don't cross this, but turn RIGHT here with a fence/hedge to your left. Continue steep-ly upwards through two fields and enter a wood. Turn LEFT along a track and follow this round to the RIGHT and then steeply uphill. Near the top cross a stile and follow the path ahead, soon going round to the LEFT next to a fence. On emerging from the wood walk straight ahead across a field, with good views to Hay-on-Wye and beyond on the left.

WALK 6

THE BEGWNS & THE WYE VALLEY WALK

DESCRIPTION This 12½ mile walk goes from Hay to Clyro and then climbs up gradually through quiet meadows and countryside to reach The Begwns. This a large (1400 acre) remote common owned by the National Trust, of much ancient historical interest and with remarkable views all round. The walk then descends to the village of Llowes (with refreshment available at the Radnor Arms) and joins the Wye Valley Walk across countryside above the Wye, finally returning along the river to Hay. **START** Hay Castle bus stop and car park, Oxford Road, Hay-on-Wye SO 230422. **DIRECTIONS** There's a direct bus service (39/39B) between Hereford and Brecon via Hay-on-Wye about once every two hours on Mondays-Saturdays, with two buses per day (39A) on Sundays. Buses from Hereford stop next to the car park; those from Brecon opposite and a few yards closer to Hereford.

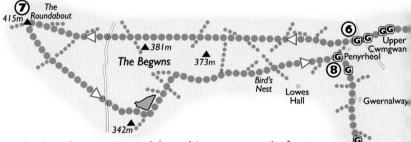

1,2&3 The first three sections of this walk are the same as for walk 8 (Cwm Byddog).

4 Walk up the road out of Clyro. About half a mile after the end of the village, ignore a left turn and continue past Cwm Cottage. Turn LEFT at the entrance to Llwyn-Celyn and follow the drive round towards the house. Bear RIGHT passing the garage on your left, go through a gate and up the right side of the field to pass through another gate. Follow the path through the wood, with a parallel lane visible down to your right. After going through another gate and continuing close to the fence on the right, you reach a gate on your RIGHT. Go through this onto the lane and continue ahead, upwards. Ignore a left fork and pass through the gate towards Lower Cwmgwannon.

5 The track goes to the left of the house; don't follow it round to a gate on the right, but go through a solid wooden gate in front, which looks like a fence but does open. Keep on through another gate, passing Great Cwmgwannon Barn on the right. On reaching two gates in front, go through the left one. Keep to the right of a house up a bank to join a track going ahead between two fences to a gate into a field. Bear slightly LEFT to the right hand corner of a hedge; continue up with the hedge on your left through a gate, then very soon through the right one of two gates. Bear RIGHT to another gate onto a road. Turn RIGHT through a gate next to a cattle grid to enter the huge expanse of common land known as The Begwns.

6 Turn LEFT, then fork RIGHT up a track. Just before a little cairn, take the second grassy track on the LEFT and walk along this, parallel to the road you can see below on the left at the edge of the common. There is no obvious path from now on, but when the road below ends keep on in the same direction. You will soon see a lake down to your left; don't go towards this, but look ahead for a small clump of trees in the far distance ahead to the right. Aim for this;

10

before long you will see that there is a stone wall round it and, just to its left, a white trig point at the highest point of The Begwns. On the way you cross a very minor road. The peak with the clump of trees is known as The Roundabout; the stone wall was built to celebrate the millennium, as was the stone seat just inside the wall.

7 On leaving The Roundabout, start back towards in the direction you came from, but after 20 paces or so turn RIGHT and head for the right hand side of the lake. Choose the least boggy route, crossing the same minor road as before, but lower down. As you approach the lake you come to a stone wall; keep to the left of this and walk round the far end of the lake. When the fence turns right, don't turn with it but keep ahead across the grass to the next fence, which you keep close to, almost back to where you entered The Begwns. A hundred yards or so before the cattle grid, you pass a large grey barn on your right. Just after this is a gate down to the RIGHT leaving the common.

8 Go through this and stay on this track through two more gates. By Lane Cottage the track becomes a road; this soon bends left but you keep ahead on a path, which you stay on all the way down until you pass a large stone house and join a road down to the RIGHT. Stay on this until it reaches a junction. Turn LEFT. Stay on this road for over half a mile to enter the village of Llowes. Near the bottom of the road turn LEFT over a weak bridge (signed), unless you want to visit The Radnor Arms, which is at the bottom of the road. Pass the church on your left to reach the main road. Turn LEFT. The rest of the route follows the Wye Valley Walk back to Hay.

9 Soon turn LEFT again at the end of a stone wall and at once RIGHT through two gates. Pass through another gate and, when the track bends to the left to a field, leave it by keeping ahead over a stile and along the top of a field. Go through a gate, past a house on the left, then through the left of two gates, and straight ahead to a hedge. Turn RIGHT in front of this passing a gateway on the left, go through a gate on the left and head diagonally down the hill to your right, passing between two areas of wood-land, to a gate onto a road. Cross the road and continue straight ahead through a gate down the field to the river. Turn LEFT. Ignore left turns until eventually you have to leave the river to the LEFT along a hedge by a house. Turn LEFT along the drive and soon RIGHT over a footbridge, past a stile and along next to a wall. Turn LEFT through a gate and go straight ahead to a gate leading to a road. Turn RIGHT back down to Hay.

11

WALK 7

KILVERT'S CLYRO

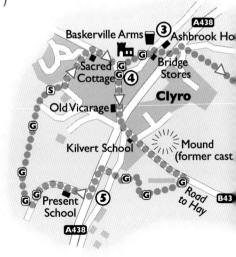

DESCRIPTION Clyro's main claim to fame is that it's where Francis Kilvert was living when he started writing his famous diary. This 5 mile walk goes over the hill from Hay to Clyro (a journey Kilvert often made) and then goes through the village past some of the places associated with him. You will also get some pleasant views of Hay and the Wye Valley from the northern, Radnorshire side of the Wye. Refreshment is available at the Baskerville Arms in Clyro.

START Hay Castle bus stop and car park, Oxford Road, Hay-on-Wye SO 230422.

DIRECTIONS There's a direct bus service (39/39B) between Hereford and Brecon via Hay-on-Wye about once every two hours on Mondays-Saturdays, with two buses per day (39A) on Sundays. Buses from Hereford stop next to the car park; those from Brecon opposite and a few yards closer to Hereford.

1 & 2 The first two sections of this walk are the same as for walk 8 (Cwm Byddog). *Kilvert wrote on April 7 1870: 'I had the satisfaction of walking from Hay to Clyro by the fields without meeting a single person, always a great triumph to me and a subject for warm self-congratulation for I have a peculiar dislike to meeting people, and a peculiar liking for a deserted road.'*

3 Turn RIGHT at the road by the Bridge Stores. *Immediately on your right is Ashbrook House, with a plaque telling you that Kilvert lived there from 1865 – 1872. Just past this is an old milestone showing the distances to Hereford and Glasbury; this road used to be the main road but it's now rather easier to imagine the village as it used to be in the 19thC. Opposite is the Baskerville Arms. In Kilvert's time it was called The Swan, and he wrote on April 12, 1870: 'Last night The Swan was very quiet, marvellously quiet and peaceful. No noise, rowing or fighting whatever and no men as there sometimes are lying by the roadside all night drunk,*

cursing, muttering, maundering and vomiting'. Turn round, walk back over the bridge and past the Bridge Stores and then turn RIGHT through a gate and go under the Yew trees to the church. Inside the church you will find some information about Kilvert and a memorial plaque to him. On leaving the church, bear RIGHT past the grave of Henry Evans on your left down to the gate.

4 Go straight ahead across the road and bear LEFT passing Stocks House on the left and, soon, The Old Vicarage on the right. *Kilvert, who was the curate of Clyro, used to visit the vicar, Mr Venables, and his wife here. On April 6 1872, 'In the afternoon I went to the Vicarage. Mrs Venables ..... came out into the garden with me and sitting under the great double-headed fir tree we talked over the evening of yesterday with reference to Daisy and myself. She told me I owed it to myself to speak to her father again.....' Kilvert was in love with Daisy, whose father, the vicar of Llanigon (walk 5), disapproved of the relationship and the pair never married. Kilvert later married someone else, but he died a month later at the age of 38. At the main road turn RIGHT and immediately LEFT (signed to Hay). Pass Kilvert's School on the right. He often came here to help with the teaching. On July 3, 1870 he wrote: 'The Government Inspector .... is coming to examine our school on Wednesday week July*

LEFT down a lane. *The last house on the right, Sacred Cottage, is an 18thC listed building which may have once been the priest's cottage.* When you reach a road, turn RIGHT. Soon bear LEFT through a gate back into the churchyard. Retrace your steps from earlier to leave Clyro – walk past the church back to Bridge Stores, turn RIGHT down to the main road, cross over and bear LEFT to a stile; once over this, walk across a field and ahead between the fences enclosing young trees. Then you can either return to Hay by the same route that you came on, or follow Section 6 below.

6 After passing between the fences, walk on to a post at the left end of a fence/hedge. Here turn LEFT across the field, with a house over down to your left. Continue to a gate, which is just in front of a small lake ahead on the left. Go through the gate. Pass the lake on your left, cross a stile and head half RIGHT up to a fence/hedge (not the one straight ahead). Walk along with the fence to your right until you reach a stile leading to a road. Turn RIGHT. After about half a mile turn LEFT back down to Hay by the road you came up earlier.

12th, so till the inspection we are working double tides to push the children on and I am going to the school 3 times every day'. Fortunately 'the children passed a good examination' on July 12. On your left you soon pass a large mound, which is the site of the former Clyro Castle, built soon after the Norman Conquest and which probably fell into ruins after the demise of Owain Glyndŵr's campaign in the early 15thC. Just past the speed limit sign, turn RIGHT through a gate into a field. Keep right and soon go through another gate ahead. Bear RIGHT to a gate just to the left of a petrol station. Walk through this and then ahead to the main road. Cross over and turn LEFT along the pavement.

5 Turn RIGHT up the next turning, which passes the present day school on your left. Follow the road round to the left and at the next drive on the right (to Little Cedars) bear RIGHT through a gate and up the left hand edge of the garden to another gate. Pass through this into a field and turn RIGHT along the bottom of the field. After going through two more gates, turn RIGHT down a track and over a stile by a gate. Soon turn

0   Miles   ¼

B4351

B4350

Wye

Hay-on-Wye

B4350

B4350

START

WALK 8

CWM BYDDOG & OFFA'S DYKE PATH

DESCRIPTION This 8 mile walk starts by going over the hill to Clyro and then takes you through woodland and countryside to the beautiful dingle of Cwm Byddog, owned by the Radnorshire Wildlife Trust. It is renowned for its ancient trees and Spring flowers. Finally you return to Hay along the Offa's Dyke Path, descending back to the Wye for the final section.

START Hay Castle bus stop and car park, Oxford Road, Hay-on-Wye SO 230422.

DIRECTIONS There's a direct bus service (39/39B) between Hereford and Brecon via Hay-on-Wye about once every two hours on Mondays-Saturdays, with two buses per day (39A) on Sundays. Buses from Hereford stop next to the car park; those from Brecon opposite and a few yards closer to Hereford.

1 From the car park entrance turn LEFT and then RIGHT to cross the zebra crossing. Continue straight ahead down the passage (Back Fold) to a road. Turn RIGHT here and walk past the castle up on your right. At the first junction turn LEFT onto a passageway (The Pavement), pass the clock tower on your left and turn RIGHT. Take the first LEFT turning (Bridge Street), cross the river and walk up the hill. Turn RIGHT at the first junction and immediately go through the second gate on your LEFT into a campsite.

2 Go straight ahead through another gate and soon cross a stile. Bear RIGHT to another stile, then go straight ahead to a gate, then bear RIGHT to another gate. Then bear LEFT diagonally down the field to a corner, through yet another gate, then straight ahead going between two fences enclosing young trees to a gate/stile. Turn LEFT and at once RIGHT across the grass to the main road. Cross over with care, turn LEFT and almost at once RIGHT along a path.

3 Turn LEFT on the road next to the Bridge Stores and then RIGHT into the churchyard through a gate. Fork RIGHT just after the church and exit through another gate. Cross over and turn RIGHT up the pavement. Pass a road called Begwyns Bluff on the left.

4 About 70 yards later leave the road over a stile on the RIGHT, walking to the left of a tarmac playing area. Follow the path into the wood over a footbridge, staying close to the stream for a short time, then turn RIGHT up to and past a stile. Climb up the slope, cross a stile on the LEFT and turn RIGHT along the right hand edge of a field. At the top pass through a gate, turn RIGHT through another, cross a stream on a few stepping stones and soon leave the wood. Bear RIGHT into a grassy patch and soon bear LEFT across a tiny stream to a gate. Go through this and head half LEFT up and across the field to a gate, which leads on to a road.

5 Keep ahead through two gates into the farm, round to the right and out through a third gate. Leave the road through the next gate on the LEFT into a field (unsigned). Cross the field to another gate about two thirds of the way down the other side; once through this continue in the same direction to another gate (the second one down), go through this and turn RIGHT down the field through two more gates to a road. Opposite is the entrance to Cwm Byddog Nature Reserve, a very pretty woodland dingle with a stunning display of wild flowers in Spring. On entering the reserve, there is a path which will take you, if you keep left all the way, through to a bench with a view over the Wye valley; on returning along this path, turnings to the LEFT will go down to the stream. Please do not stray off the paths. On leaving the reserve, turn RIGHT on the road and walk for about 200 yards to the first gate on the LEFT. Go through this (unsigned), turn half RIGHT, ascend to the opposite corner and cross a stile. Keep to the right hand edge of the field, cross another stile and continue round to the LEFT until you get to a stile on your RIGHT. Cross this, and another, to reach a road.

6 Go straight ahead along the road. Turn into a field through the second gateway on the RIGHT. Keep to the right side of the field through another gate and on to exit through two more gates on to a road. Turn LEFT, taking care on this relatively busy short stretch of road. Turn RIGHT at the next junction. In about ten minutes turn RIGHT to go down steps as you join the Offa's Dyke Path (signed),

0   Miles   ½

Tump Farm

Bettws Dingle

Cwm

Crossfoot Farm

7

Lower Wernypentre

Upper Wernypentre

A438

Cwm Byddog Nature Reserve

5

Entrance to Nature Reserve

Offa's Dyke Path

Penllan

Wye

3 A438

4

Clyro

through a gate, cross a muddy track and go through another gate into a large field. Bear LEFT across the field to the opposite side, go through another gate in front of you, then slightly RIGHT across the field and through yet another gate. Turn LEFT along a track; at the end turn LEFT and at once RIGHT with a hedge on your right. Pass through a gate and continue ahead, soon next to the River Wye on your left. After passing through two more gates and some woodland, go up steps to reach a road. Turn LEFT over the bridge and retrace your steps to the car park and bus stops.

which you follow all the way back to Hay. Cross the stream and then ascend to walk along the right hand side of the wood. Leave the wood through a gate, passing through another gate to join a track, where you turn RIGHT to the main road.

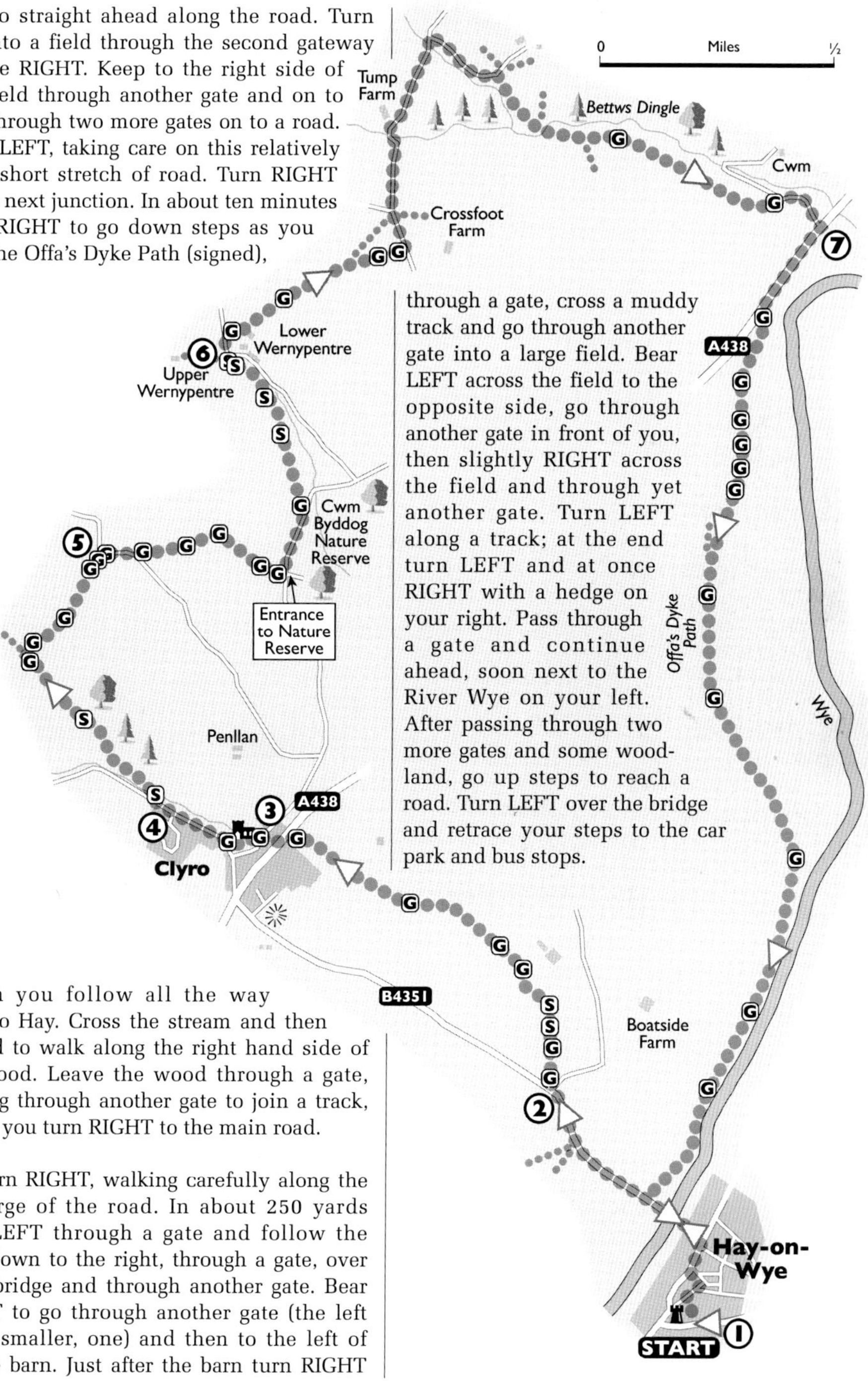

B4351

Boatside Farm

2

7 Turn RIGHT, walking carefully along the verge of the road. In about 250 yards turn LEFT through a gate and follow the path down to the right, through a gate, over a footbridge and through another gate. Bear RIGHT to go through another gate (the left hand, smaller, one) and then to the left of a large barn. Just after the barn turn RIGHT

Hay-on-Wye

START **1**

15

SATURDAY 25 JULY 2020

WALK 9

ROUND THE EDGE OF HAY-ON-WYE

DESCRIPTION There are plenty of attractive paths very close to the centre of Hay, which many visitors are unaware of. This 3½ mile walk takes you on some of them and is a good way of filling an hour or two if you want a breath of fresh air. The views of the hills may also tempt you to try some of the other walks in this book that go further afield.

START Hay Castle bus stop and car park, Oxford Road, Hay-on-Wye SO 230422.

DIRECTIONS There's a direct bus service (39/39B) between Hereford and Brecon via Hay-on-Wye about once every two hours on Mondays-Saturdays, with two buses per day (39A) on Sundays. Buses from Hereford stop next to the car park; those from Brecon opposite and a few yards closer to Hereford.

I Walk down to the bottom right hand corner of the car park and through the gate in front of you. Keep to the right hand edge of the field and leave it over a footbridge to go through two gates to a road. Keep LEFT here and immediately turn RIGHT onto a track passing to the left of a grey barn. Turn RIGHT through a gate and bear RIGHT across the field towards the hedge on the right hand side. Walk through a gateway ahead. Bear slightly LEFT with the hedge, then slightly RIGHT to pass through another gate(way). Continue straight ahead to go through another gate. This takes you onto Hay Common, which is Open Access land, so you can continue forwards and wander over the common.

2 If not exploring the common, ignore the waymark pointing ahead and do a U-turn to your RIGHT through a gate next to a stream on your left. Follow the path as it crosses four footbridges in succession, so the stream is again on your left. Continue down to the road; as you approach it you will see that the stream is mysteriously on

your right by now! Turn LEFT and cross over with care. Immediately after the Cartref Residential Home on the right, turn RIGHT down a narrow path. Turn LEFT at the next road. Just after the last house on the right and before the road narrows, turn RIGHT (signed as a Bridleway).

3 Follow the track, which after a while passes between the walls of the old railway bridge and on through a gate to a meadow. *This meadow is known as The Warren; it has been used as a recreation area by the people of Hay for many years. At one time there was a proposal to turn it into a caravan park, but local residents bought the field so that it could continue as a meadow. It may in medieval times have been used to breed rabbits (hence the name); it's now an area of Special Scientific Interest.* Walk down to the river and turn RIGHT. Leave The Warren through a gate and follow the path ahead. Soon after passing Warren Cottage on your right, turn RIGHT through a short tunnel and walk up the path. *On your right is St Mary's Church; the tower is 15thC, but most of the church was restored in the 19thC. It's clear as soon as you enter that it's emphatically Anglo-Catholic nowadays.*

4 If not visiting the church, turn LEFT on the pavement at the end of the path and very soon turn LEFT again past a stone bench. *The mound on your right is the Motte of the old Motte and Bailey castle dating from about 1100.* Descend the steps and walk along the path with the stream on your left. At the end turn LEFT between a stone bench on your right and wooden railings on your left. On your left is a small waterfall. After looking at the waterfall, turn round and either turn RIGHT along the wide track, or go down steps ahead to your left and then turn RIGHT to rejoin the path you left when you turned off through the tunnel. *The wide track goes along the old railway line, originally a tramroad from the Monmouthshire & Brecon Canal which became the Hereford, Hay and Brecon Railway in 1863 and closed 100 years later. The narrower path is the Bailey Walk, which was laid out for the people of Hay by Sir Joseph Bailey in 1884. There are several* places where you can transfer from one to the other. The two paths join up before long, just after the Bailey Walk goes through a gate.

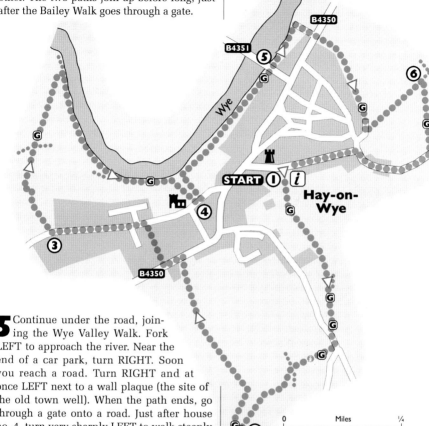

5 Continue under the road, joining the Wye Valley Walk. Fork LEFT to approach the river. Near the end of a car park, turn RIGHT. Soon you reach a road. Turn RIGHT and at once LEFT next to a wall plaque (the site of the old town well). When the path ends, go through a gate onto a road. Just after house no. 4, turn very sharply LEFT to walk steeply downhill. Cross a footbridge and then walk through a gate to climb up the bank next to a house. Turn RIGHT, keeping in the centre of the field.

6 In front of a gate leading to a stream, turn sharp RIGHT, leaving the Wye Valley Walk, and walk across the field to a gate, through which you exit the field. *On your right is a Village Hall.* This may surprise you, as Hay is hardly a village. However, when you crossed the stream a few minutes ago you crossed the border over the Dulas Brook into England and you are now in Cusop, a small Herefordshire village. Walk ahead to the road and turn RIGHT. The road crosses the Dulas Brook back into Wales and then winds back to the car park and bus stops.

Hay-on-Wye

TUESDAY 28TH JULY 2020

WALK 10

MOUSE CASTLE WOOD & THE WYE VALLEY WALK

DESCRIPTION This 7½ mile walk starts off by climbing through Mouse Castle Wood, owned by the Woodland Trust and renowned for its ancient oak trees. The next stage involves gently undulating countryside as far as the remote hamlet of Priory Wood, where in summer you can visit a picturesque tea garden. You return to Hay by a pretty route along the Wye Valley Walk (WVW).

START Hay Castle bus stop and car park, Oxford Road, Hay-on-Wye SO 230422.

DIRECTIONS See Walk 9 for directions. If coming by bus, it would be more convenient to get off two stops from Hay Castle on the Hereford side at the bus stop close to where the 30 mph speed limit starts; look for the turning on your left (if coming from Hay) called Nantyglasdwr Lane; if you do this, ignore the first two sentences in Section 1 below.

1 From the Hay Castle bus stop/car park walk along Oxford Road towards Hereford passing a turning on your left (Bell Bank). Continue on the main road for about half a mile until you pass Nantyglasdwr Lane on your left. About 100 yards beyond the lane turn RIGHT over a stile. Cross a small stream; turn half LEFT in the field to a stile; cross this and keep ahead along a slight dip in the ground to another stile by a telegraph pole leading to a road. Turn LEFT and then RIGHT at a T junction. In about 250 yards turn LEFT through a kissing gate. Walk straight ahead up to the corner of the field and over a stile into the woods. Follow the path, keeping right at a junction. A little later, bear LEFT up steps. Ignore a right turn down to a stile and soon turn RIGHT out of the wood through a gate.

2 Cross a track and turn LEFT over a stile, then keep next to the hedge/fence on your left to the end of the field. Pass through a gate. Turn RIGHT and at once bear LEFT to walk down towards a farm. Aim for the bottom end of a row of about 15 trees. Go through the gate beyond the trees; turn half RIGHT to another gate. Cross the drive and turn LEFT through a third gate, then RIGHT through a fourth. Turn half LEFT down to the corner of the field. Cross a stile to a road. Turn RIGHT and immediately LEFT over another stile. Follow the left hand side of the field and at the bottom turn LEFT over a stile. Cross a plank bridge. Stay on the right side of the field, ignoring a stile to your right. Cross a stile ahead and walk over a grassy patch past a house on the right. After another two stiles you reach a road. Cross this with care.

3 Cross a stile just to your RIGHT. Aim slightly RIGHT through the field and look for a stile just to the right of a telegraph pole. Cross the stile and a footbridge and head half LEFT up the slope to cross another stile. Go ahead at about the same height to a hedge and a gate. Turn RIGHT before the gate and keep the hedge on your left up the field until you reach a stile on the LEFT. Cross this and turn half RIGHT to go through a gap and on in the same direction to a stile/gate onto a road. Turn LEFT, then RIGHT at the junction.

4 Soon bear RIGHT across a small common towards an old chapel. Cross the road and a stile next to a VR letter box. Keep ahead through a gate just to the right of stables, then to a stile at the bottom of the field leading to a road. Turn LEFT and at once RIGHT through a gate/stile into a field. Keep to the left next to woodland and at the bottom cross a stile onto a road. Turn RIGHT. Follow the road until you get to Walkers Cottage on your left. *In fine weather you can visit the tea garden here and enjoy a drink and a home-made cake; it's nearly always open from April to October but at other times phone in advance (01497 831684/07522 442124). The route then continues along the road for 300 yards or so.*

Opposite Pool Pardon cottage on the left, turn RIGHT over a stile, joining the WVW (which you stay on back to Hay).

5 Walk ahead, crossing a footbridge with a stile at each end and, later, two more stiles to reach a road. Cross this and go up the grass to another road. Turn RIGHT. Opposite the chapel bear LEFT across the common to another road. Turn LEFT. At the next junction leave the road by walking straight ahead through a gate; soon cross one stile and then turn half RIGHT to go over a second. Walk down the field to join a track on your LEFT, which takes you to a road. Turn LEFT, then, at the second gateway, RIGHT over a stile.

6 Follow the hedge on your right through a gate and round to the LEFT over one stile, then another, to reach a stream.

course. Eventually the path leaves the woodland by veering to the LEFT through trees and crosses the drive to the former clubhouse on your left. Leave over a stile; soon cross a footbridge and stile, then another stile

and go through a gate, with Hay clearly in sight ahead to your right. Aim slightly RIGHT through the field to another gate, then on over three successive stiles to a lane.

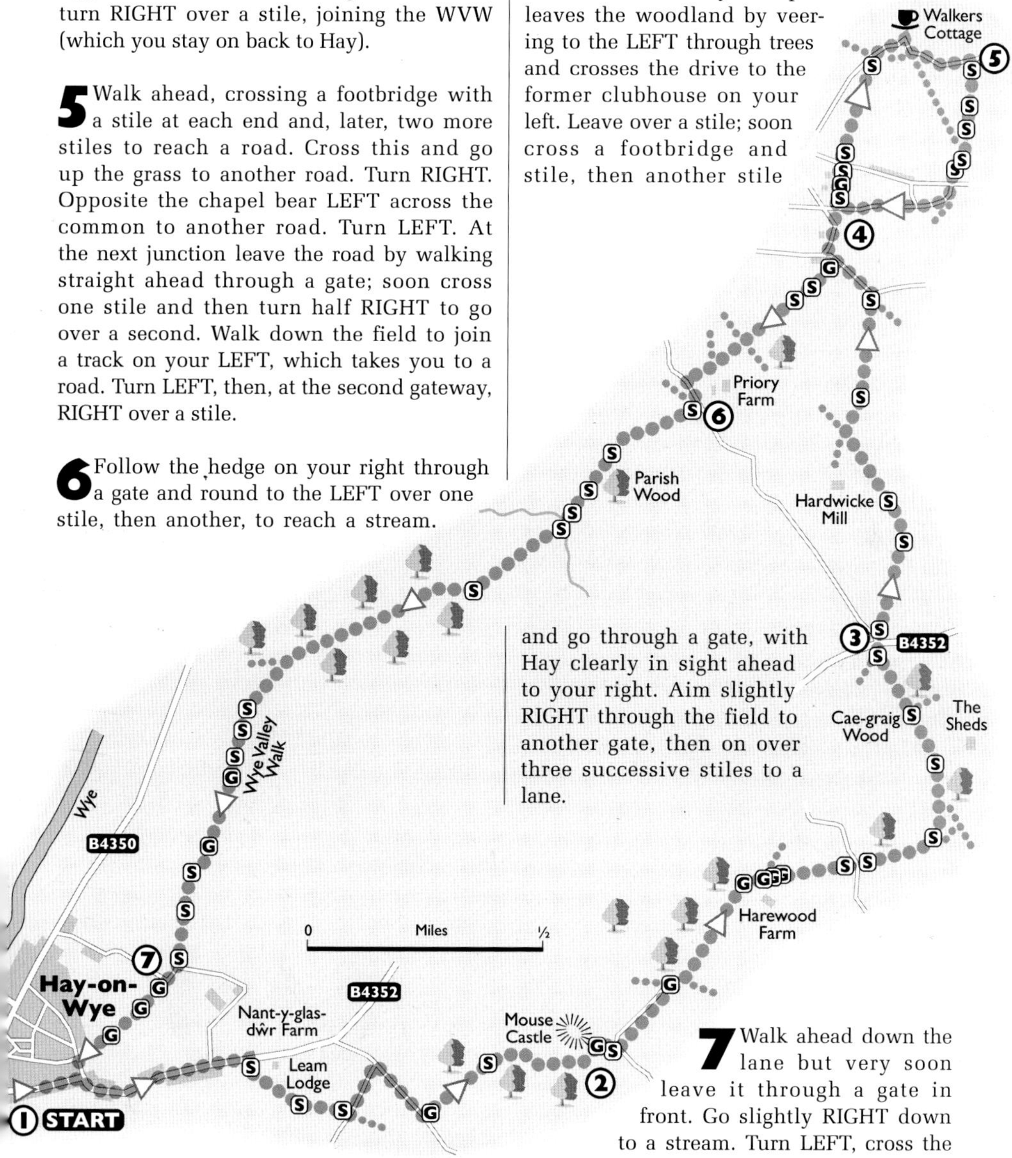

7 Walk ahead down the lane but very soon leave it through a gate in front. Go slightly RIGHT down to a stream. Turn LEFT, cross the stream and turn RIGHT through a gate. Walk straight across the field and down a bank just to the left of a house. Pass through a gate and over a footbridge and climb up the short steep stretch of road to a junction. Here the WVW turns right, but you go ahead, soon turning LEFT into Lion Street, then RIGHT back to the start.

Cross this by a footbridge with two stiles and keep ahead with the hedge to your left. When the hedge bends to the left, keep straight ahead, crossing a stile. Turn RIGHT at the second post and follow the path down and round to the LEFT close to woodland on your right, along the edge of a former golf

Map labels: Walkers Cottage, Priory Farm, Parish Wood, Hardwicke Mill, B4352, Cae-graig Wood, The Sheds, Harewood Farm, Wye Valley Walk, B4350, Hay-on-Wye, Nant-y-glas-dŵr Farm, B4352, Leam Lodge, Mouse Castle, START, Wye, Miles

WALK 11

CUSOP DINGLE, NEW HOUSE WOOD & CEFN HILL

DESCRIPTION This is a varied and beautiful 9½ mile walk which starts off following the very picturesque Dulas Brook through Cusop and beyond. It goes through attractive woodland, before climbing up and along the top of the isolated common land of Cefn Hill, with spectacular views. It then goes back for a short time into woodland and finally comes back through remote shady countryside down to Cusop Dingle and back to Hay. If visibility is poor, *do not* attempt this walk as you may get lost on the top of Cefn Hill (and will not see the views).

START Hay Castle bus stop and car park, Oxford Road, Hay-on-Wye SO 230422.

DIRECTIONS There's a direct bus service (39/39B) between Hereford and Brecon via Hay-on-Wye about once every two hours on Mondays-Saturdays, with two buses per day (39A) on Sundays. Buses from Hereford stop next to the car park; those from Brecon opposite and a few yards closer to Hereford.

1 Walk down to the bottom right hand corner of the car park and through the gate in front of you. Head slightly LEFT to the opposite corner of the field and go through a gate, joining Offa's Dyke Path (ODP). Keep along the right hand edge of the field to pass through another gate. Here leave the ODP by turning LEFT. Go through a gate, over a footbridge and along a path; when it ends, turn LEFT and then RIGHT onto a road. Walk along this for over a mile until the road ends, then continue ahead through a gate past Brickyard Cottage on your right, and on in the same direction over a stile, through a field and into a wood. The track gradually rises into the wood; ignore paths down to the right. The path gets narrower and passes a waterfall. At a fence in front, the path does a large U-turn RIGHT over the stream and up the other side, soon leaving the wood over a stile.

2 Keep next to the wood on your right until you reach the very ruined remains of an old house. Immediately past this, turn LEFT up the hill, passing a tree with a yellow waymark. About 40 paces later, turn RIGHT across the meadow; soon you will see a house in the distance in front of you slightly to the right, and you will pass well below buildings uphill on the left. Join a track going towards the house, but when this starts descending veer LEFT to cross the field steadily ascending to a stile behind and just to the right of a patch of bracken. Cross this, turn RIGHT, then RIGHT again through a gate, soon forking slightly LEFT along a path passing close to a house on your right. The path stays next to the fence on your right for some time, then crosses it via a stile, soon crossing back over another stile. Keep ahead and over another stile until you get to a junction with a forest track. Here turn LEFT. AT the next crossing of tracks turn RIGHT down a grassy path, ford a stream and follow the path round to the RIGHT and over a much smaller stream. Cross a stile and a footbridge. Keep ahead through the trees and, on emerging into a field, turn LEFT to the highest point of the field. Keep ahead to a stile onto a road. Turn LEFT.

3 Just after the end of trees on your left, turn LEFT onto a track with a gate on each side. Immediately turn through the one on your RIGHT (no waymark, and very few from now until section 4) and head half LEFT up the field to the far corner. Pass through the gate, then at once through the second gate on the RIGHT. Keep next to the fence on your right as far as a gate in front of

20

you; once through this, continue on the track until, just in front of a gate to a farmyard, turn LEFT up a steep slope and walk with the fence to your right for a short distance to reach a farm track. Turn LEFT up the track, passing a gate on your right. Stay close to the telegraph poles, go through a gate and continue next to the poles until there are two between you and the fence ahead.

4 Here turn LEFT along a grassy track. The track is very indistinct in places, but aim for the top of the ridge and continue in the same direction without descending to right or left; this last instruction is important! Keep the radio mast over to your right in view; if you lose sight of it you've gone too far to the left. Eventually the track descends gently to a gate in front, which is the way into the wood. Pass through this and walk ahead; at a junction turn RIGHT, then immediately LEFT, and at the next junction continue down in the same direction to a T-junction with a road.

5 Turn LEFT. When the wood ends, pass a turning and footpath to the left and in a few minutes turn LEFT over a stile close to a gate. Aim slightly LEFT down the field, soon going

to the left of a little stream. Look across the stream to your right and, in about 100 yards, when you see a gate and stile across the field turn RIGHT to ford the stream and aim for the gate and stile. Cross the stile and walk towards trees slightly to your LEFT. Keep to the right of the trees and soon pick up a good track going down through them. Pass a ruin on the left and, just before another on the right, turn RIGHT up some very old steps and then LEFT behind the ruin. Keep ahead on a narrow path to a stile, then follow the fence on your left, before long through bracken. When the fence turns left, head slightly RIGHT up the path, but soon descending. Go down a few steps and turn RIGHT. Cross a stile by a gate, keep near the bottom of the field to another stile, then descend half LEFT to a gate leading into a farmyard. Walk past the house, then bear LEFT down the tarmac drive to a road. Turn RIGHT. You can now either return to Hay on the same route that you came on, or you can take a different route back by following stage 5 of walk 12 (Henallt Common).

Tycoch · Cusop Dingle · Dulas Brook · Graigau · New House · New House Wood · Meardy Dingle · Cefn Hill · Abbey Farm · Miles 0 ½

HENALLT COMMON,
TACK WOOD & CUSOP DINGLE

DESCRIPTION This walk takes you on some relatively little used footpaths to some beautiful and empty countryside south of Hay. The 6 mile walk involves a stiff climb up to Henallt Common, an area of wooded grassland designated as a Site of Special Scientific Interest and with good views over to Hay and beyond. It then goes through peaceful woodland and finally descends back to Hay via the delightful Cusop Dingle – supposedly the last place in Britain where fairies were seen. There is one very boggy patch, and there are streams to be forded.

START Hay Castle bus stop and car park, Oxford Road, Hay-on-Wye SO 230422.

DIRECTIONS There's a direct bus service (39/39B) between Hereford and Brecon via Hay-on-Wye about once every two hours on Mondays-Saturdays, with two buses per day (39A) on Sundays. Buses from Hereford stop next to the car park; those from Brecon opposite and a few yards closer to Hereford.

I Walk down to the bottom right hand corner of the car park and through the gate in front of you. Head slightly LEFT to the opposite corner of the field and go through a gate, joining the Offa's Dyke Path (ODP). Keep along the right hand edge of the field, through another gate and ahead to, and through, a third gate. Here leave the ODP by turning half RIGHT and walking diagonally across a small field. Cross a stile by a gate and continue straight ahead, soon skirting a barn, to another stile in the next corner. Cross this. Turn LEFT and, in about 40 yards, just before the entrance to a farm, turn RIGHT up some steps and over a stile. Turn LEFT and walk along the edge of the field to another stile; cross this and another a little way ahead, and then a third ahead and slightly to your LEFT. Then keep next to the wood to your left and continue in the same direction until you reach a stile leading to a road.

2 Once over this, turn LEFT and soon cross a stream. Immediately turn RIGHT through a gate into a field. Keep close to the stream on your RIGHT and quite soon turn RIGHT to cross a stile and a footbridge over the stream. Bear LEFT into a field and head up the field to a hedge on your RIGHT, and on next to the hedge to the corner of the field. Cross a stile and continue close to the hedge, soon crossing another stile into woodland. Keep ahead, soon fording the stream on your LEFT and going up into a field. Keep ahead to a gate quite near the bottom of the field, go through this and turn LEFT. Turn RIGHT through the first gateway, then LEFT up the left hand edge of the field. At the top cross the stream and continue ahead, up steeply through trees to a fence, where a stile (slightly to your left) takes you into a field. Head slightly RIGHT uphill towards the left hand end of a grey barn. Before you get to the barn, cross a stile and turn LEFT on a lane.

3 The lane bends round to the RIGHT; then at once turn LEFT, going behind barns and a house through gates. Follow the path along a boardwalk and then ahead, ignoring a (signed) right turn up steps. Your route crosses another boardwalk. *You are now on Henallt Common, an SSSI which is home to a wide variety of plant life, including the rare meadow saffron, also known as autumn crocus.* Keep to the right near woodland, soon picking up a clear path which crosses four more boardwalks to reach a road. Turn RIGHT to climb steeply, then more gently, passing a stile on the left where the ODP joins your route. Continue through a farm and into woodland. Cross a stream and soon turn LEFT through a gate, leaving the ODP. Turn RIGHT at once and stay on the clear path through the wood. At a wide forest track turn RIGHT and at once LEFT and down, through a gate and out of the wood. This stretch can be very wet. When you reach a ruined house, turn RIGHT in front of it and go along a wide tree-lined track, getting closer to a stream on the left. Pass through a gate and turn LEFT to cross the stream; then bear LEFT up the bank to a fence. Turn RIGHT to a road.

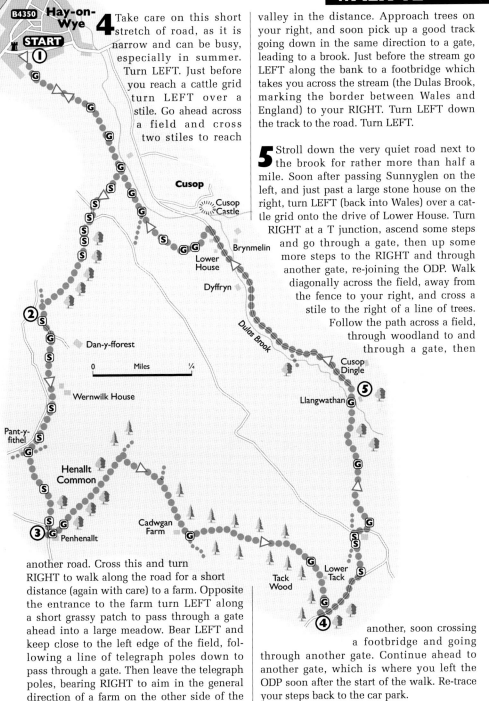

4 Take care on this short stretch of road, as it is narrow and can be busy, especially in summer. Turn LEFT. Just before you reach a cattle grid turn LEFT over a stile. Go ahead across a field and cross two stiles to reach valley in the distance. Approach trees on your right, and soon pick up a good track going down in the same direction to a gate, leading to a brook. Just before the stream go LEFT along the bank to a footbridge which takes you across the stream (the Dulas Brook, marking the border between Wales and England) to your RIGHT. Turn LEFT down the track to the road. Turn LEFT.

5 Stroll down the very quiet road next to the brook for rather more than half a mile. Soon after passing Sunnyglen on the left, and just past a large stone house on the right, turn LEFT (back into Wales) over a cattle grid onto the drive of Lower House. Turn RIGHT at a T junction, ascend some steps and go through a gate, then up some more steps to the RIGHT and through another gate, re-joining the ODP. Walk diagonally across the field, away from the fence to your right, and cross a stile to the right of a line of trees. Follow the path across a field, through woodland to and through a gate, then

another road. Cross this and turn RIGHT to walk along the road for a short distance (again with care) to a farm. Opposite the entrance to the farm turn LEFT along a short grassy patch to pass through a gate ahead into a large meadow. Bear LEFT and keep close to the left edge of the field, following a line of telegraph poles down to pass through a gate. Then leave the telegraph poles, bearing RIGHT to aim in the general direction of a farm on the other side of the

another, soon crossing a footbridge and going through another gate. Continue ahead to another gate, which is where you left the ODP soon after the start of the walk. Re-trace your steps back to the car park.

ALMELEY

DESCRIPTION An easy 6 mile walk through gentle countryside, with several orchards, a dingle (with climbs and fallen trees; this requires agility), half timbered houses and a mile or so of quiet lane walking. Eardisley is renowned for its black and white houses. In the 1980s it offered village weekend breaks where visitors stayed in villagers' homes; the Black and White Trail was also conceived by the late David Gorvett at that time. Almeley is equally charming with a fine church and castle mound. Refreshment is available at The Bells, Almeley (also a shop) and also at The New Strand (café, bookshop and bar) and the Tram Inn at Eardisley.

START Eardisley, Tram Square, SO 311496.

DIRECTIONS There are four buses a day from Hereford to Eardisley on Mondays-Saturdays (446 and 462); they operate from Hereford Country Bus Station to Tram Square. Alight at Almeley Road, Eardisley. There is limited on street parking in Eardisley.

From the front entrance to The New Strand go LEFT and LEFT again along the Almeley Road to the edge of the village. At this point, go LEFT through a gate into a large field. Follow the hedge on the right as it curves RIGHT, but look out for a well-worn path LEFT across the field to a small gate. Go through and walk ahead, near a line of trees, towards the top of the field, but beforehand cut RIGHT to drop down a bank to a footbridge (this should be treated with care and one at a time) across a brook into Holywell dingle. *Managed by the Herefordshire Nature Trust, this woodland is a joy in Spring when the wood anemones and bluebells are in full flower.* This section is nearly a mile in length and can get muddy. The path rises up the bank ahead (quite steeply in places) to a junction by holly bushes. Turn LEFT here for about 100 yards to another junction where you peel off LEFT to descend into the valley bottom again. Keep RIGHT to cross a stile and then follow the path winding its way up the dingle with a brook to your left. It climbs again up steps and down steps; ignore a bridle gate on the left, keeping ahead again to a junction. Head

slightly RIGHT to climb up the hillside and past a finger post. Continue ahead.

2 Eventually you come to a stile. Cross it, climb another stile by a signpost, then go RIGHT over a third stile through a gateway into a field. Head diagonally across it to the far corner, and go over a footbridge into an adjoining field. Turn LEFT and go through a gate onto a track. Keep RIGHT to proceed along the track through New House farm buildings, through a gate on to a road.

3 Cross over and proceed ahead through two barred gates in the field. Continue with the hedge on the left and cross two stiles to enter the grounds of Nieuport House, an eighteenth century hall which is listed. *It is said that in earlier centuries Sir John Oldcastle, who led an ill-fated uprising against the Crown and Catholicism in the early 15thC, resided in a medieval house on the same site.* Walk ahead between a dingle on the right and a pool on the left. At the end of this green dam, look for a gate on the RIGHT. Go through and head diagonally across a large field towards an old lodge house. Cross a stile onto a drive and go RIGHT. At the road turn RIGHT and then go LEFT opposite the old lodge to cross a stile.

4 Follow the hedge to cross a stile, then ahead to a gate and stile on the RIGHT at the field corner. Go over it and keep LEFT to cross a stile near two gates. Once over, head slightly RIGHT to climb a stile by a barred gate in the next boundary. Proceed in a similar direction, across the next field to a gate and stile which leads onto a road. Cross over and climb a stile by a double gate into an orchard. Head slightly LEFT to cross a stile by a gate into a field and continue in a similar direction to climb a stile in a hedge and in wet ground. Keep ahead to descend to a stream, across a footbridge and stile. Walk onward by the earthworks of Almeley Castle on the left. Cross a stile onto the road by the church. *The church dates from the 13thC with many additions through the late medieval period. Nearby is the Manor House, a 16thC timber framed dwelling interlaced with brick (not open to the public).*

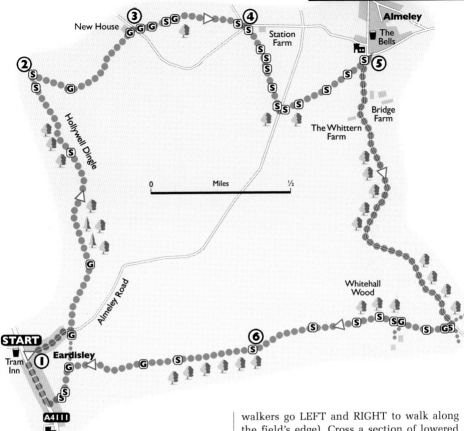

5 If you are visiting the Bells go LEFT; it's a very friendly place to take refreshment. Otherwise, go RIGHT and follow this lane for about a mile to Lower Newton farm; you'll be near when the road weaves by houses. Opposite barns, turn RIGHT over a stile and keep ahead. There's a dwelling to your left. Go through a gate into a field and head slightly RIGHT to pass a veteran oak. Cross a stile by a gate into an orchard and proceed in the same direction. Go through a barred gate, left of a red brick house, over a track and cross a stile. Now head slightly LEFT by a large oak to a stile in a hedge. Cross it and walk ahead between trees in the orchard. Climb a stile in the next hedge and now go LEFT and RIGHT to walk down the field by the hedge on the left. Cross a stile and head slightly LEFT across the next field (although some local walkers go LEFT and RIGHT to walk along the field's edge). Cross a section of lowered fencing. In the next field, aim for the far LEFT corner where there's a footbridge.

6 Once over, go slightly LEFT over a stile and then head slightly LEFT towards a fence then ahead alongside a wood. Cross a stile in a hedge and head slightly RIGHT now through wet ground to and through a barred gate over the line of the old Eardisley to Titley Junction railway line. Head slightly LEFT to a footbridge. Follow the hedge as it curves LEFT to cross a footbridge and onto the old tramroad. Go LEFT and then RIGHT through a gate into a pasture. Head diagonally across to a stile. Cross it and then another to the RIGHT. Go ahead on the pavement, across a road and between houses into Millstream Gardens to reach the main A4111 in the village. Turn RIGHT to return to Tram Square.

WALK 14

BRILLEY

DESCRIPTION An easy 8 mile walk through undulating countryside to Brilley; there are one or two short climbs on this section. The walk passes Eardisley church, known for its historic font, described by Pevsner as 'the most exciting piece of the Norman school of Herefordshire, for composition and even more for preservation'. Brilley is in a very isolated part of Herefordshire, feeling more akin to Wales than England; this is true border country. The walk follows parts of the Herefordshire Trail. Refreshment is available in Eardisley at The New Strand (café, bookshop and bar) and the Tram Inn.

START Eardisley, Tram Square SO 311496.

DIRECTIONS There are four buses a day from Hereford to Eardisley on Mondays-Saturdays (446 and 462); they operate from Hereford Country Bus Station to Tram Square. Alight at Almeley Road, Eardisley. There is limited on street parking in Eardisley.

From the entrance to the Tram Inn go RIGHT to walk down the main road to the parish church. Go RIGHT by the church; the road bends LEFT and RIGHT to pass a community orchard and by the earthworks of Eardisley Castle. There's now a straight road through to Eardisley Park standing on the left – *a fine example of a Queen Anne House, beautifully restored after a fire in the 1990s and using mainly the original bricks.* Beyond the house, the lane kinks LEFT and RIGHT to pass barns and houses to become a green bridleway. Go through a gate and onto a field path ahead with a hedge to the left. On reaching the road by the kennels go LEFT. Follow this to a crossroads at Millhalf.

2 Go straight across and at the junction before Millbank turn RIGHT to descend

to another junction where you keep RIGHT. The road rises and bends to the left by a dwelling called the Vallets. Just beyond, go RIGHT to cross a stile by an old track. Head towards the telegraph pole, ahead through a gateway, and then LEFT up to cross a stile into Kiln Ground Wood. Now go ahead to reach a junction where you turn RIGHT and within 20 yards go LEFT to walk through the wood to a stile. Cross it, then walk ahead along a bank to climb a stile by a gate into the hamlet of Little Merthyr.

3 Go RIGHT on the road to a junction where you turn LEFT. Climb up to a second road junction and go LEFT again but within 150 yards turn RIGHT to cross a stile. Go slightly LEFT over a stile into a wood. The paths bends LEFT and is narrow and littered with leaves so neat footwork is required. *This is Brilley Green Dingle, a semi natural woodland managed by Herefordshire Nature Trust.* Go RIGHT over the footbridge and follow the track ahead as it climbs the side of the dingle to pass Brilley Court Farm, a 17thC farmhouse of architectural beauty. Go through a gate, then proceed ahead, but as the track bends slightly left and there's a fork to the right, go sharp RIGHT up steps (easily missed!) to cross a stile. Walk ahead through a small orchard and cross another stile. Aim very slightly RIGHT in the next field towards a large yew to enter the churchyard through a kissing gate. *Brilley's simple rural church is a delight; it was refur-*

bished in the 19thC. Walk ahead to a gate leading on to a road.

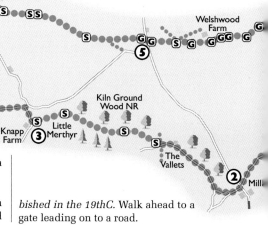

26

4 Go LEFT to leave the hamlet, ignore a road to the right, and at the crossroads of tracks go RIGHT through a gate. Keep ahead with a hedge to the left, ignoring a stile to the left. At the next boundary climb a stile and continue ahead again to cross a double stile and footbridge. Proceed ahead with the hedge to your left alongside an old sunken track and by a corrugated iron shed. You will soon reach a waymark post where you go LEFT over a stile into an adjacent field. Turn RIGHT and as you pass to the left of a cottage head slightly LEFT across the field towards barns. Go through a gate onto a road.

5 Turn RIGHT and then go LEFT through the second gate on the left. Head slightly RIGHT aiming to the left of a bungalow. Cross a stile onto a track and pass to the left of the bungalow. Just beyond, go through a gate on the RIGHT. Welshwood farm is to the left. Head slightly LEFT to a corner of a hedge and keep LEFT through a gateway (with sheep hurdle). Proceed through a gate with a house and garden on the left to anoth-

along you will come to a waymark post. Cut RIGHT here across the field to a gateway on the other side. Now head slightly LEFT in the next field, cross a stile in the fence and aim for the houses, coming alongside a hedge on the left (ignore the stile there) and ahead to climb a stile onto a road in Woodseaves.

6 Go LEFT through the hamlet and look for a path off to the LEFT after a red brick cottage. Follow the track up to a gate. Go through into a field, turning RIGHT to walk along the field's edge. Cross a stile and then head slightly LEFT up the field, through a bridle gate and ahead to cross a stile by a wood. Cross it and aim slightly RIGHT in the next pasture. Go over a stile and keep RIGHT to cross another. Head slightly LEFT across the next field to a stile. Climb over it and continue in a similar direction to a stile adjacent to a gate onto a road.

7 Turn LEFT and follow the road to a junction by Pound Farm. Go RIGHT here, then ahead at the next junction and LEFT at the third. As the road bends right, go RIGHT over a stile. Walk ahead, climb a stile and continue ahead again to cross a third stile to walk between gardens and

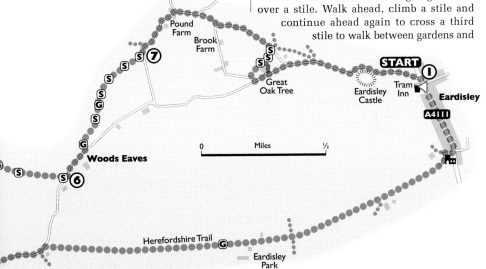

er gate. Once through, head slightly RIGHT across a field and through a gate in a hedge. Turn LEFT. Go through a barred gate and keep ahead along the field's edge. Half way

an old cemetery to a road. Go LEFT to pass by the Great Oak, estimated to be at least 600 years old and some arguing that it is possibly 900 years old. At the junction turn LEFT to walk back into Tram Square.

BREDWARDINE

DESCRIPTION A strenuous 6 mile walk over Dorstone Hill, passing by the ancient burial site of Arthur's Stone with its enormous capstone and walking by the parish church of Bredwardine, where the diarist Francis Kilvert was rector from 1877 to 1879. There are steep climbs but the views are spectacular. Refreshment is available at Dorstone's Front Room (mornings only), the Pandy Inn at Dorstone and the Red Lion Hotel at Bredwardine.

START Pandy Inn, Dorstone SO 313417.

DIRECTIONS There's a direct bus service (39) between Hereford and Hay-on-Wye via Dorstone about once every two hours on Mondays-Saturdays, with three buses per day (39A) on Sundays. They all stop by the village green in Dorstone. There's a little parking available by the village hall in Dorstone, opposite the Green, and also a small amount of on-street parking near the Green.

I Standing with your back to the entrance to the Pandy Inn go LEFT and then RIGHT at the village green then RIGHT again along Chapel Lane. Turn LEFT at a junction and walk to the B4348. Go RIGHT to walk on the road but be wary of traffic as you rise up to Lower Crossway Farm; it is best to be on the left hand side of the road before it bends sharp right at the crossroads. Your way is ahead up a drive to pass Crossway farm and ahead on a track rising to a gate. Go through here and ahead to a stile just beyond the gate in the hedge. Cross it and turn LEFT to climb on a track up the hillside over three stiles by gates. Continue ahead to cross a stile to Arthur's Stone monument. *This Neolithic burial chamber is associated with a fanciful tale about a tussle between King Arthur and a giant.*

2 Go to the LEFT of the monument and cross the road. Go over the stile by a gateway into a field. Keep ahead along the field's edge, then cross a stile by a gate into the next field. Aim slightly RIGHT across a field to a stile by a gate. Cross the stile, proceed ahead to cross another in the next boundary, then slightly RIGHT to climb another stile. Go RIGHT to walk near the hedge on your right to a corner where a stile is seen to the right. Do not go over but cut LEFT instead keeping near the fence on the right and by ruins of Bottrell farm to a stile. Climb this and go LEFT to descend to another stile. Cross it and walk through wet ground, curving LEFT along the hillside to a corner by a wood with a stile beneath trees. Cross it and head slightly LEFT down the hillside (steep here) to a gate.

3 Go through and keep slightly LEFT to pass through a gate and wet ground. Head slightly RIGHT with a hedge to the right. Continue through a bridle gate (ignoring the stile) and continue slightly RIGHT on an old track by the hedge as it curves down through to pass through another gate. On the right is Wern Wood Nature Reserve. Turn LEFT and go through a gate down to a road. Go LEFT and at the main road, cross over and turn LEFT. Pass a veteran oak and then go through a gateway on the RIGHT along a hedge on the left. Cross a stile on the LEFT to walk along boardwalks and by several ancient trees before going through a gate. *This is the site of Bredwardine castle, scant earthworks which include old fishponds.* Keep ahead as the path winds through the wood and then runs alongside a hedge to the left, through a gate and onto a track by Bredwardine church. Kilvert's grave can be found in the churchyard.

4 Go LEFT to the road and turn LEFT on a road into the centre of the village. Across the road stands the handsome 17th century Red Lion Hotel. Cross the road and walk along a track between the Red Lion on the right and a farm on the left. The track rises to a gateway. The track peels off to the RIGHT here and the path runs ahead, alongside a hedge in a garden next to a half timbered house. Cross a stile to re-join the track. Some locals skirt the garden by walking along the track which peels RIGHT and then LEFT to this point. Either way you go ahead through the gate on the RIGHT into a pasture where you head diagonally across to find two stiles. Go ahead here (rather than left) to cross a stile into the dingle, over the stepping stones in a small stream. After 20 yards the path climbs slightly RIGHT out of the dingle, over a plank bridge, rising again steeply, finally going up steps to cross a stile onto a green track. Go LEFT for the road.

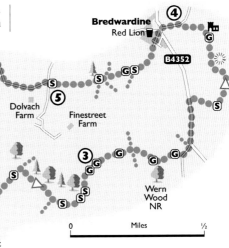

tage. Cross a footbridge and a stile. Head slightly LEFT to climb alongside a wood and look to ease away slightly RIGHT by a sole tree up the pasture to a stile in a hedge. Cross it and continue ahead to climb a stile by a gate. Now head slightly LEFT to pass conifers to a gate. Once through, keep ahead to exit on to a road through double gates.

6 Go RIGHT to walk along the road. At the junction, go LEFT, signposted to the Bage. Pass a drive leading off to the right and as the road descends look for a stile halfway down. Go LEFT to cross it and continue ahead to join a track. Go LEFT on the track through a gate and then onwards towards Llan Farm. By the first barn, cut LEFT over a stile into a field and turn RIGHT. Cross a stile and head slightly RIGHT to a third. Once over turn LEFT and at the junction turn RIGHT down a green lane, over a stile, and then another to join Spoon Lane.

7 Go LEFT along it but look out for a stile on the RIGHT. Cross this into a field and head slightly LEFT across it to a footbridge and steps up over the Golden Valley railway track bed. Cross a stile to a recreation ground. Head slightly LEFT to join the hedge and ahead to the main road. Cross with care and walk on a path alongside the churchyard to a road. Keep ahead along Church Lane to the green.

5 On the road, turn RIGHT and then LEFT at the junction signposted to Arthur's Stone. Rise up the lane, between newly planted orchards towards Crafta Webb; the road bends RIGHT and then LEFT. Look for a track by a signpost which peels off LEFT before after a stone house and before a cot-

1 From the bus stop at Vowchurch Turn cross the road with care and walk down to the Church, seen on the left in a serene setting by the River Dore. Continue on the road into Turnastone, passing by Turnastone Court Farm – *part of the Countryside Restoration Trust and including water meadows untouched for centuries. Note the simple medieval church on the right and traditional shop/garage on the left.* The road bends RIGHT and runs by some houses; as it bends left keep ahead through a barred gate into a field.

2 Continue alongside the hedge, through a gate into a pasture and ahead again through a succession of pastures passing

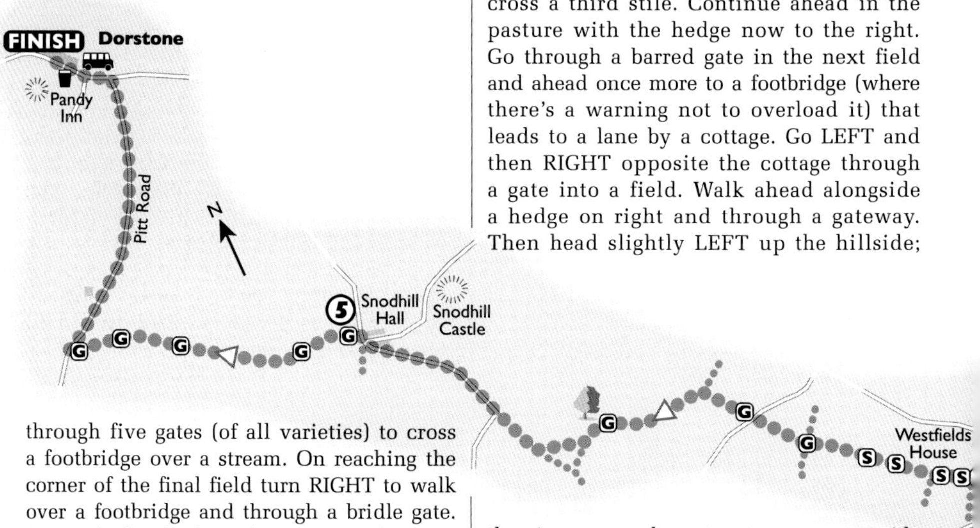

FINISH Dorstone

Pandy Inn

Pitt Road

N

5 Snodhill Hall / Snodhill Castle

G G G ▷ G G

G △ G

G G S S Westfields House

S S

through five gates (of all varieties) to cross a footbridge over a stream. On reaching the corner of the final field turn RIGHT to walk over a footbridge and through a bridle gate. Proceed ahead, through a gate in the next boundary and ahead again to reach a bridle gate and on the RIGHT a footbridge over the watercourse. Once over, go LEFT on the track and RIGHT over a stile. Head slightly LEFT across the field by a stand of conifers. Cross a stile by a hollybush and walk over the old trackbed of the Golden Valley railway and through rough ground to cross a stile onto a lane. Go RIGHT over the bridge and then LEFT over a stile into a pasture. Walk alongside the river at first and then aim slightly RIGHT towards the houses. Exit over a stile on to the B4348 in Peterchurch. Walk along the pavement to the Boughton Arms.

3 At the Bougton Arms, turn LEFT to pass St Peter's church on the left; cross the bridge over the River Arrow and then a path bends LEFT and then RIGHT over the old trackbed of the Golden Valley Railway once again. Follow the track ahead to a lane into Hinton. Go RIGHT and ahead at Hinton crossroads.

4 Just before a cottage, turn LEFT through a gate into a field. Follow the hedge on the left, cross two stiles in succession (but ignore the one on the left). Pass through the top of an old orchard and proceed ahead with a hedge to the left. Cross a stile in the next boundary, and then onward over another stile and through a small belt of trees to cross a third stile. Continue ahead in the pasture with the hedge now to the right. Go through a barred gate in the next field and ahead once more to a footbridge (where there's a warning not to overload it) that leads to a lane by a cottage. Go LEFT and then RIGHT opposite the cottage through a gate into a field. Walk ahead alongside a hedge on right and through a gateway. Then head slightly LEFT up the hillside;

there's a waymark post part way up to guide you towards the far top left corner by the wood. Here you join a track in the woodland, through a gate, and then follow the track as it bends RIGHT and descends the hillside to a road. Turn RIGHT to walk into the hamlet of Snodhill, over a footbridge by a ford and then climbing up to a crossroads.

5 Continue on the road as it curves RIGHT for a few yards and turn LEFT on a farm track, often muddy, to proceed through a barred gate. Continue on the tractor track to a second barred gate and keep ahead with a hedge to the right. Walk through another gate and ahead to cross a small stream and through a fourth gate. Continue ahead along a green rim curving LEFT to a stream and then on a track to a bridle gate and lane. Turn RIGHT here to walk into Dorstone along Pitt Road and in the village turn LEFT for the Pandy Inn and village Green if you need to catch the bus back.

WALK 16
VOWCHURCH TO DORSTONE

DESCRIPTION This is an easy 5½ mile linear walk, following for the most part the Herefordshire Trail. There are very few climbs. The walk passes the quiet villages and hamlets of Vowchurch, Turnastone and Snodhill as well as the larger settlements of the valley, Peterchurch and Dorstone. There are refreshments at Peterchurch (Boughton Inn and Nags Head public house and at Dorstone the community run Front Room (coffee, tea and cakes) and the Pandy Inn.

START Vowchurch Turn, SO 364367.

FINISH Pandy Inn, Dorstone SO 313417.

DIRECTIONS There's a direct bus service (39) from Hereford or Hay-on-Wye to Vowchurch and Dorstone about once every two hours on Mondays-Saturdays, with three buses per day (39A) on Sundays. The walk starts at the bus stop at Vowchurch Turn. At Dorstone buses stop by the village Green. There's a little parking available by the village hall in Dorstone, opposite the Green, and also a small amount of on-street parking near the Green, where you could catch a bus to Vowchurch for the start of the walk.

St Peter's

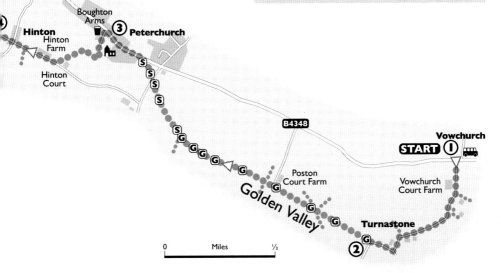

31

BIRCHY HILL

DESCRIPTION This 4 mile moderate walk takes in very quiet country over Stockley Hill where there are exceptional views across Herefordshire to the Malvern Hills and across the Golden Valley to the Black Mountains. The outward route passes by Wellbrook Manor in Peterchurch which, according to Pevsner, is 'one of the best surviving examples in the county of a 14thC hall-house'. Refreshment is available at the Boughton Arms or the Nag's Head, Peterchurch.

START Boughton Arms, Peterchurch SO 345386.

DIRECTIONS There's a direct bus service (39) from Hereford or Hay-on-Wye to Peterchurch about once every two hours on Mondays-Saturdays, with three buses per day (39A) on Sundays. They all stop by the Boughton Arms in Peterchurch. Car parking is available opposite St Peter's church, just off the B4348.

1 From the entrance to the Boughton Arms, go ahead along the main street toward Hereford to a crossroads. Turn LEFT her-esigned towards Stockley Hill. As the road bends left and you see the ancient yew hedge of Wellbrook Manor on the left, go RIGHT as signposted before stone garages through a barred gate. Head slightly RIGHT towards a hedge but then turn LEFT at the waymark post up an old sunken track which rises to a gate. Go through it and keep ahead for about 10 yards before turning LEFT over a stile.

2 Proceed ahead along a line of trees, on the right side, up the bank to a gate. Go through it and walk ahead towards the corner then cut RIGHT up to the brow and walk ahead up to the top RIGHT corner where you cross a stile to the right of a barred gate. Continue ahead with a hedge to the right and alongside a wood to go through a gate. Keep ahead across a large field as the wood peels off to the right. Cross a stile and a stone step stile. Ignore the gate and stile on the left. Go ahead to enter a wood and follow the track as it weaves ahead near to the fence on the left and with old workings to the right. The track leaves the wood, through a gate into a field. Keep ahead with a hedge to the left, go through another gate ahead (dwellings seen across to the left). The path now follows the field's edge ahead, then RIGHT until it curves around to a stile. Cross it and go LEFT and LEFT again on a track offering lovely views across Herefordshire. The track joins the road at Stockley Hill.

3 Go LEFT to climb up to the aptly named Bank House on the right. Go next RIGHT, through a gate and proceed on a track running along a ridge towards Lyonshall Barn (a dwelling) which you soon pass. Go through a gate into Rough Leath wood and walk along the forestry track. The track descends and bends to the right and at this point peel off LEFT on a lesser woodland track at the waymark post. There are timber extractions so cross new tracks emerge from time to time. However, keep ahead to cross two tracks but after the second, look for another smaller track in about 10 yards easing away to the LEFT. Follow this lower track which soon rises and forks RIGHT beneath tall conifers. Keep ahead until it reaches a junction near to a fence where you cut LEFT and RIGHT to follow a wet path which begins to curve to the LEFT of Rough Leath barn.

4 The track reaches a gate to exit the wood. Do not go through it. Stay on the path which continues to curve LEFT through the wood and which soon descends near to the fence on the RIGHT and exits into a pasture. Once through go LEFT to drop down to go through a gate and then ahead to go through another which enters the woodland. The path follows the woodland edge of Oakes Coppice; the path then bends RIGHT and LEFT to a go through a gate and into a pasture. Keep ahead with a hedge to your LEFT, by gorse bushes and through a gate. Go ahead and then LEFT to follow a line of trees and a sunken lane which bends LEFT. It then joins a wider track, often muddy in

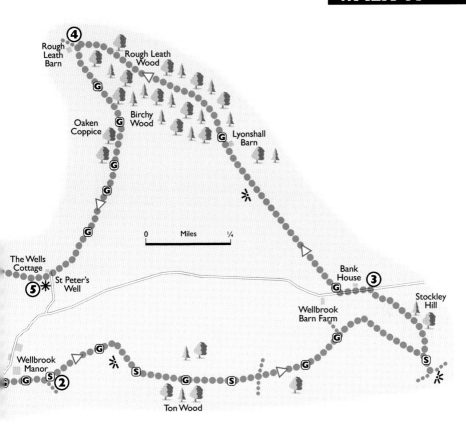

winter, with a stream to the LEFT and by a derelict building. Proceed through a gate to descend in a wood and keep ahead at a junction with a dwelling to the RIGHT.

5 The path runs ahead beneath a hazel and holly canopy. Once again, you might find this to be very wet after rainfall so be pre-

pared. Pass by a cottage on the RIGHT and then turn next LEFT to drop down RIGHT to Bazley farm where you go LEFT at the junction. Follow the track ahead to re-enter Peterchurch near the Boughton Arms.

Wellbrook Manor

MICHAELCHURCH ESCLEY

DESCRIPTION A moderate 8 mile walk across borderland pastures where farmers have reared sheep for centuries. This includes Shepherds who produce very tasty ice cream made from sheep's milk; it is on sale at their shop and café in Hay. There are splendid views over the Golden Valley and Black Mountains throughout the walk and two highlights, the Bridge Inn at Michaelchurch Escley and the haunting ruins of Urishay Castle.
START Boughton Arms, Peterchurch SO 345386.
DIRECTIONS There's a direct bus service (39) from Hereford or Hay-on-Wye to Peterchurch about once every two hours on Mondays-Saturdays, with three buses per day (39A) on Sundays. They all stop by the Boughton Arms in Peterchurch. Car parking is available opposite St Peter's church, just off the B4348.

1 Standing with your back to the Boughton Arms go ahead along the main street in Peterchurch. Pass Closure Place, then cross a stile on the RIGHT into a field. Head across it and to the far right corner where you cross a stile onto a road. Go RIGHT and once over the bridge go LEFT over a stile through rough ground (site of the old Golden Valley Railway line) to cross another stile. Aim slightly LEFT across a large field by conifers to a stile in the far corner. Once over go LEFT and RIGHT over the footbridge.

2 Go through two gates here to continue ahead with the Trenant stream to the right, then the path curves RIGHT between a hedge on your left and a large group of alder trees on the right. Cross a stile in the top corner by a barred gate. Walk up the hillside near a wood to the right. Cross a stile and continue upwards through a gate. Aim to the RIGHT of the barns in the next field. Just to the RIGHT of them, go through a gate and continue ahead along a track, with a hedge to the left, going through another gate and

pasture to reach two gates. Go through the one on the LEFT and then cut RIGHT with the hedge to your right. Cross a stile into the next field and approach Dolward farm. Continue ahead to go through a gate on the left and proceed along a track between hedges to the farm buildings.

3 Go through three barred gates by the farm; ignore the track waymarked to the right, but instead go ahead and through a gate on the LEFT. Walk down the hillside with the farmhouse garden to the left. As the hedge cuts left continue down to a gate. Go through this, step across the small stream and now head slightly LEFT up the bank. Join a hedge at a corner and proceed ahead through a gatethen go slightly RIGHT to cross a stile by a holly bush. Head slightly RIGHT. Pass by the second telegraph pole from the left and look to the RIGHT of a barred gate where you cross a stream and stile. Continue ahead with a hedge to the left. Ignore the gate on the left but head slightly RIGHT to go through bracken and ahead across a drive to a footpath signpost near a stone house.

4 Turn RIGHT to climb the hill. Ignore the first road off left and continue ahead at the second junction by the chapel. However, before the road bends, go LEFT through a gate into a pasture behind houses. Head slightly RIGHT and aim for the far top corner to the LEFT of the end house. Exit onto a lane, turn LEFT and then in 50 yards go RIGHT along a track to reach two gates. Go through the one on the LEFT and follow the hedge on the right to another gate. Go through and proceed with a hedge on the right to pass through a gate into the next pasture. Aim slightly LEFT down to a gate. *The view across to the Black Mountains is splendid and you'll also catch sight of the church at Michaelchurch Escley with its distinctive pyramid tower.* Walk down the pasture to cross a stone stile by a gate. Head slightly LEFT through another gate and then go slightly RIGHT along a hedge on the right to descend, steeply at the bottom, to a stile and a road by the Bridge Inn. *You could take a break at this superb hostelry.*

5 On the road, turn RIGHT and RIGHT again at the first junction and RIGHT at the second. Pass Bank Farm, then a few trees as you climb up the hillside. As the road bends right go LEFT through a gate into a field. Walk ahead along a track, through a gate and ahead again alongside a wood on the right. Pass through another gate and then keep ahead across the next field to a gate, then bear LEFT across a corner of a field to a gate into a wood. The track descends to the RIGHT, then winds down LEFT and RIGHT to pass through another two gates. Go RIGHT in the pasture up the bank but within 150 yards go slightly LEFT to climb parallel

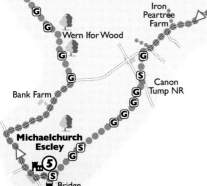

to a tree belt to the left of barns (official diversion). Continue ahead through two gates and over a summit. Head slightly RIGHT aiming for a gate to a road.

6 Turn LEFT and then RIGHT at the junction. Follow the road for about half a mile, past a turn on the right for Urishay Court and a telephone kiosk. At the next junction, cross a stile on the RIGHT, walk down to cross another stile. Aim just LEFT of the farm

buildings and you can see the ruins of Urishay Castle. *This early castle motte earthworks are crowned with the remains of 17thC house; it is private property.* Exit through a gate onto the road. Go RIGHT and descend to a stream and scrub land.

7 As you begin to rise, look for a double gate on the LEFT and the footpath sign. Go through the gates and rise up the field with a hedge to the right. Cross a stone stile between gates and then continue to reach the summit. Cross a stile and walk ahead in the next field to climb a stile. Now head slightly LEFT down a steep bank to cross a stile beneath a large oak. Cross it and turn RIGHT to pass through a hedge and onward through a gate into an old orchard. Continue towards the rear of a dwelling. Cross a stile and pass down the drive to a road. Go LEFT and RIGHT at Hinton crossroads and walk ahead to the Nag's Head public house, which is open all day. At the main road go RIGHT to walk into Peterchurch.

35

1 From the bus stop at Vowchurch Turn cross the road with care and walk down to the church in a serene setting by the River Dore. Continue on the road into Turnastone, passing by Turnastone Court Farm – *part of the Countryside Restoration Trust and including water meadows untouched for centuries. Note the simple medieval church on the right and traditional shop/garage on the left.* The road bends RIGHT and within 100 yards look for a stile on the LEFT. Cross it and walk straight ahead through a long pasture. Cross a stile in the boundary and proceed ahead at first then aim very slightly RIGHT to a gate in the top far right corner. Go through it onto a road.

2 Turn LEFT on the road. Ignore the first turning left but rise up to a few houses at Slough Bridge. Just before the road bends left go LEFT over a footbridge, proceed ahead in a pasture and through a barred gate into Slough Breast Wood. The path turns LEFT and rises to curve gently RIGHT to a stile. Climb

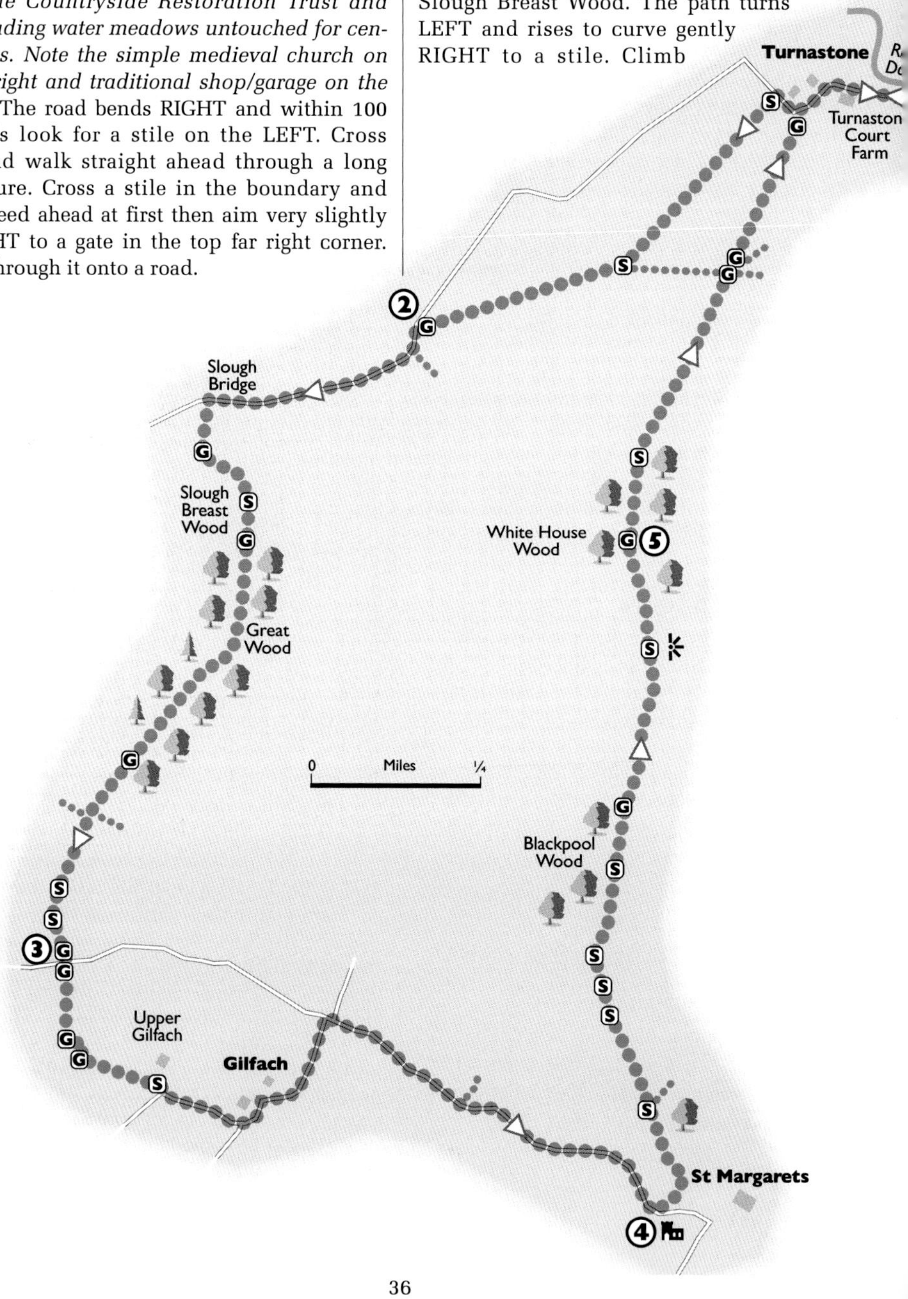

Turnastone

Turnaston Court Farm

②

Slough
Bridge

Slough
Breast
Wood

Great
Wood

White House
Wood **⑤**

Blackpool
Wood

0   Miles   ¼

③

Upper
Gilfach

Gilfach

St Margarets

④

ST MARGARETS

DESCRIPTION A moderate 6 mile walk through a very quiet corner of Herefordshire to St Margarets, including one of the loveliest sections of the Herefordshire Trail. The walk starts in the sleepy village of Vowchurch, passes through Turnastone and then across pastures and woodland to sheep grazing territory around Gilfach. The main feature is St Margaret's church with its rood screen, noted by Pevsner as 'one of the wonders of Herefordshire'. There are no refreshments available on this walk; there is a café and pub at Poston Mill in Vowchurch which is open on a seasonal basis.

START Vowchurch Turn, SO 364367.

DIRECTIONS There's a direct bus service (39) from Hereford or Hay-on-Wye to Vowchurch about once every two hours on Mondays-Saturdays, with three buses per day (39A) on Sundays. The walk starts at the bus stop at Vowchurch Turn. There is a small amount of on street parking near the church.

this and head very slightly RIGHT to a gate to enter Great Wood; the path is often muddy here in winter. Continue ahead to climb through the wood, cross a track and continue to make your way up between tall trees. The path veers LEFT, but ignore the turning to the left here. Keep ahead to exit by way of a barred gate. Head slightly RIGHT to the top right corner of the field and continue ahead with a hedge to the left. Cross a double stile and proceed to cross a footbridge on the left. Go RIGHT to along a hedge to pass through a barred gate onto a road.

3 Cross the road to go through a barred gate into a field. Walk ahead to pass by the ruin of a barn and across a stream to go through another barred gate. Follow the fence on the LEFT and then turn RIGHT to a third barred gate. Go through and walk ahead to cross a footbridge and stile; Upper Gilfach farm stands to the left. Go RIGHT on the drive and then turn LEFT to walk down to another junction. Turn LEFT and rise up to a third junction at Shobdon Barn. Go RIGHT to walk through to St Margarets. *The beautiful church with its square bell turret stands to the RIGHT next to Tanhouse Farm. The rood screen was built in the early 16thC and is an amazing survival given that there was a purge on this sort of ornate feature during the Reformation. The wall texts are from the 18thC including one at the entrance as you leave: 'Go and sin no more'.*

4 Return to the road and then turn RIGHT through a gateway and up a track by outbuildings. Then turn LEFT in a small enclosure to rise up and continue between trees along a green lane. Cross a stile by a gate at the end with a superb view towards the Grey Valley. Head slightly LEFT down the hillside to a stile leading into a small coppice. Cross it and walk through to cross another stile. Head across a pasture to climb a third stile. Now dip down to a stream and rise up a bank aiming slightly LEFT to a stile at the edge of Blackpool wood. Go over it and head RIGHT. The path winds through the wood, with some waymarks to assist route finding, eventually to a gate. Go through it and keep ahead to pass through a patch of woodland with a hedge on the right. Exit through a stile into the next pasture and then ahead to Chanstone wood.

5 Go through a gate and choose the lesser path on the LEFT to descend to cross a stile and head slightly RIGHT through scrub to a field. Head diagonally across the field; go through a gate in the far RIGHT corner (to the left of a tractor bridge). Go through a barred gate and now head slightly LEFT towards a white cottage. Go through a gate to join a track to the road and then turn RIGHT to retrace your steps through Turnastone to Vowchurch.

WALK 20

ROWLSTONE

DESCRIPTION This moderate 3½ mile walk follows paths and lanes in the south eastern end of the Golden Valley from Pontrilas, where the Golden Valley Railway at one time departed from the main line for Hay-on-Wye. The main feature is Rowlstone church, which historians suggest has some exceptional examples of the Herefordshire School of sculpture. In the summer months, make time to call at the café at Rowlestone Court for farmhouse ice cream; the views are also good from this point. In the second part of the walk the paths descend to Ewyas Harold and meander along the Dulas brook back to the start point, altogether a pleasant experience. There's refreshment available at Ewyas Harold, at a café at Pontrilas Timber and also at Pontrilas Post Office.

START Telephone Exchange bus stop, Pontrilas SO 398276.

DIRECTIONS There's a direct bus service (X4) from Hereford, Abergavenny or Cardiff to Pontrilas about once every two hours on Mondays-Saturdays. There is limited on street parking in Pontrilas.

I Facing the bus shelter at the telephone exchange, go RIGHT to walk along the pavement through the village. *On the left you'll see Pontrilas Court, a listed building with decorative windows, dating from the 17thC.* Walk down to the bridge over the confluence of the Dulas Brook and River Dore. Cross over the road at the bridge and continue to the main road. Cross with care as the road can be busy. Go LEFT on the pavement to reach the turning on the RIGHT for Rowlstone. Pass the entrance to Pontrilas Timber and then look for a stile on the RIGHT.

2 Cross this and head diagonally across the field. Proceed through a kissing gate onto a track and walk along it until it bends to the right. Go through a gate on the LEFT here, and once through, turn RIGHT to walk ahead in the field, then step over a plank bridge and through a barred gate. Continue

ahead with woodland to the left and a works and house to the right. In the field, aim slightly LEFT to climb up to the top far left corner. Cross a footbridge and stile and walk through the wood; the path bends slightly LEFT through to another stile by a gateway. Cross the stile and head slightly RIGHT to pass to the left of a clump of trees and pool. Keep ahead, passing to the left of a veteran oak tree, to reach a barred gate. Go through and continue ahead again to exit through a kissing gate onto a road.

3 Turn RIGHT on the road (and RIGHT again to Rowlestone Court café if you are stopping). *This leads to the beautiful church of St Peter on the right, a must for all those interested in the work of the early Romanesque style work of the early Norman artisans of the time.* The road bends RIGHT and then LEFT by Church Farm. Turn RIGHT at the junction on the road signposted to Longtown. This climbs up to a cottage. Just after, go RIGHT on a lesser road which descends beneath oaks and offers good views across Herefordshire. It becomes a track (and a drainage channel too) as the road bends left to a dwelling. Walk down a couple of yards then go RIGHT to climb up over a stile into a field.

4 Go slightly LEFT across the field to the far left corner. Climb a stile and proceed ahead alongside a hedge on the left until you reach a stile on the left. Cross this and walk through the wood to exit at a stile on the other side. Now turn LEFT to walk alongside the wood in a field. At the end, cross a stile and ditch onto a track then turn LEFT. Walk down for about 100 yards; go through a gate on the RIGHT onto an old track. Go over a stile and then cut LEFT over another to enter a field. Head diagonally across the field, the tall poplars offer a landmark. *From here you*

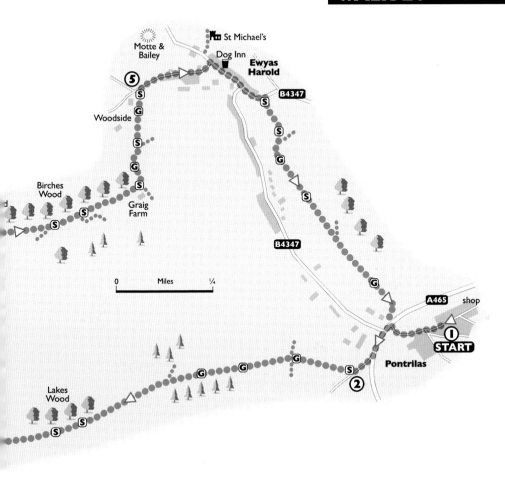

can see the sizeable castle motte towering over the village of Ewyas Harold, built by William FitzOsbern, a stark reminder of the subjugation of resident population by the Normans in the 11thC. Go through the small gate to the left of a barred gate and head down the field alongside the fence to cross a stile by the Footpath sign to the road.

5 Go RIGHT and walk into the village, passing the Dog Inn, Temple Bar and a fish and chip shop so there's considerable temptation. You will also see the church of St Michael on the left, which has a number of interesting monuments from differ-

ent ages. Continue along the pavement to the roundabout and keep LEFT here on the B4347 to pass a chapel. Cross the road with care and go up a drive, by the signpost, to cross a stile into a field. Go ahead to cross another stile and then aim slightly RIGHT to a footbridge across the Dulas Brook, home to the rare white clawed crayfish. Do not cross the bridge, but go LEFT through the gate and ahead along the field's edge to climb a stile into a larger pasture. Follow the path through to a bridle gate by the sewage works. A track leads ahead to the main road at Pontrilas. Cross with care to retrace your steps back through the village.

39

PRONUNCIATION

Welsh	English equivalent
c	always hard, as in **cat**
ch	as in the Scottish word lo**ch**
dd	as th in **then**
f	as f in o**f**
ff	as ff in o**ff**
g	always hard as in **got**
ll	no real equivalent. It is like 'th' in then, but with an 'L' sound added to it, giving 'thlan' for the pronunciation of the Welsh 'Llan'.

In Welsh the accent usually falls on the last-but-one syllable of a word.

KEY TO THE MAPS

 Walk route & direction

──── Road

•••• Adjoining path

Ⓖ Gate

Ⓢ Stile

⚐ Viewpoint

Church

Chapel

∼∼∼ Stream

Trees

+++++ Railway

Bridge

THE COUNTRYSIDE CODE

• Be safe – plan ahead and follow any signs

• Leave gates and property as you find them

• Protect plants and animals, and take your litter home

• Keep dogs under close control

• Consider other people

Open Access

Some routes cross land where walkers have the legal right of access under the CRoW Act 2000. Access can be subject to restrictions and closure for up to 28 days a year. Please respect any notices. Visit www.ccw.gov.uk for more information.

Published by **Kittiwake-Books Limited**
3 Glantwymyn Village Workshops, Glantwymyn, Machynlleth, Montgomeryshire SY20 8LY

© Text & map research: Les Lumsdon & Mike Ledlie 2014
© Maps & illustrations: Kittiwake-Books Ltd 2014
Drawings: Morag Perrott
Cover photos: Main: Arthur's Stone. *Inset:* St Mary Magdalene, Eardisley. David Perrott

Care has been taken to be accurate.

However neither the author nor the publisher can accept responsibility for any errors which may appear, or their consequences. If you are in any doubt about access, check before you proceed.

Printed by Mixam Print, Leeds.

ISBN: **978 1 908748 22 5**